THE
SUCCESS
FACTOR

THE
SUCCESS
FACTOR

Sidney Lecker, M.D.

Facts On File Publications
New York, New York • Oxford, England

Library of Congress Cataloging-in-Publication Data

Lecker, Sidney.
  The success factor.

  Includes index.
  1. Success. I. Title.
BF637.S8L425 1985   158'.1   85-16135
ISBN 0-8160-1271-7
Printed in the United States of America

Composition by Facts On File/Circle Graphics
Printed by R.R. Donnelley & Sons, Co.
10 9 8 7 6 5 4

CONTENTS

Part I

Part II

■ INTRODUCTION
Success, You Say

Success gives some people a rush, others a rash. Some of us just can't win for losing. Take Charles, a graphic artist highly regarded in his field. Is he a success? By the standards of his boss he is. But by his own judgment he's a failure.

"Call me successful?" Charles said to me one day. "If not having enough money and failing in all my long-term relationships is being a success, then I guess you could say I'm a winner."

"What about the rest of your life, Charles?" I asked.

"Oh, yes, my friends think I'm doing great. The logos I design are seen everywhere. I have lots of prestige. And my boss would give up his Rolls and firstborn before letting me go. But I'm not successful by my own standards. Isn't that what counts?"

Charles was right, partly. While it's important to be successful by your own standards, we are judged as being successful or not by many criteria.

Take the case of Noreen. As a twenty-eight year old, Noreen was content in her life. Recently a mother, Noreen had what many young women would desire—marriage to a successful lawyer, a varied and interesting group of friends, a new, healthy baby and a life in an upscale community. But, while Noreen judged herself to be highly successful, her husband did not. He left her for a woman of the same age who was creative director of an ad agency. While her husband, Colin, had serious problems of his own, we will focus here on Noreen and her plight.

Noreen was broken and indignant when we first met and she told me how Colin had announced he was going to leave her.

"Just like that he tells me he wants to trash what took us eight years to create. I thought he was building a life with me that he wanted too. We made joint decisions on everything, including on when I would give up my career in order to start a family. Then he tells me he's 'lost respect for me' and can't live with someone he can't admire."

I tried to calm her and explore their problem at the same time. "Was there a time when things started to unravel?" I inquired.

"I swear," she shot back, "he did this with no warning. I went from model wife to future ex-wife in an instant. It's disgusting, what he's done."

Noreen was right to be indignant. But her husband's loss of respect for her shouldn't have surprised her. He was an over-achiever who was attracted to her in college because she was one too. She was beautiful, a star of the college debating team and had a 3.7 GPA. When she graduated, she started work in marketing and was on a fast track from the start. No wonder Colin was dazzled by her, especially given his values. No wonder he lost interest when she gave it all up to live a restricted life, doing his bidding and taking care of their child. Colin may have acted like a cad, but Noreen was also quite naive. Being successful was important to both of them when they met. She should have suspected that trouble might arise based on the fact that Colin's concept of success did not include Noreen being a housewife. Success is in the eye of the beholder. It doesn't matter what others think of your life and your success, as long as you don't depend on them for anything (an impossibility unless you intend to live as a fur trapper or fisherman). Because most of us live in a complex society, we are judged and rewarded personally and professionally by others. Consequently, we must have a personal success goal that is consonant with that of the others we interact with and depend on. This isn't called "compromise," it's called "reality." My definition of success must please not only me, but also those important to me, or I may suffer the fate of a Noreen. Conversely, going too far in the other direction is dangerous too. Trying too hard to please others and forgetting to develop your own definition of success will destine you to a fate such as Charles's—impressing everyone else and yet being personally miserable. Somewhere there is a happy medium.

Being successful, like throwing darts, requires that you see the bull's-eye if you're going to score. You need to have inner goals for your success, like Noreen did. And you need to know what others need from you and establish targets to be met there too, like Charles was able to do.

How do you know where to begin? Are there some people more likely to be well-rounded successes than others? "Can I be one of them?" you ask.

The Success Factor

For many years, the behavioral sciences (psychiatry, psychology and sociology) were preoccupied with deviance. What was mental illness? How did it come about? What social factors caused criminality? So intense was this preoccupation that these sciences left normality and what creates it completely out of the picture. That this should have happened isn't surprising. The "medical model" was strongly influential in the origins of these sciences. We know that medicine is more concerned with how to cure illness than how to create and maintain health. This is no great slur on the reputation of doctors. They have been too busy curing us over the decades to step back and study what we should do to make ourselves healthy. Interestingly, the movement for preventive medicine, including nutrition, exercise and life-style management to control stress, had very strong roots in industry. Corporations, for the sake of economics, are very concerned with keeping their people healthy. And so, industry has championed the practices of annual check-ups, wellness programs and the like.

In the field of mental health, industry has also been keenly interested in prevention for many different reasons. Management wants to keep people healthy in view of the intense emotional stress of high performance. Companies simply can't afford to have a big producer burn out. Certain other industries have been justifiably concerned with security and have commissioned studies to have "profiles of unreliability" developed so that security risks could be identified before any damage might be done.

I have been deeply involved in studies, devising ways to predict unreliable people before they are hired and divert them away from security-sensitive environments. It was from this background in behavior prediction that I first became interested in developing a profile for the prediction of "success behavior." I thought, "Surely if we can design techniques to identify and foil airline hijackers or saboteurs, we can go the other way, identifying people who are destined to succeed." I embarked on a quest for such a technique several years ago, beginning with a massive search of the existing literature.

For those who are unfamiliar with research technique, the first step in any research project is to define the state of the art. Thanks to the existence of computers and on-line data bases, it was possible to search the world literature for any and all research papers that dealt with predicting success. One gives the computer a command that identifies the topic and tells the brilliant microchips that the search should be "wide" rather than "narrow," meaning, "Give me all the data and, if you're not sure something is relevant, include it anyway." Not blinking its red light-emitting diodes even once, the computer set off on its mission, returning a few hours later with several thousand references on all manner of "successes."

Culling through these, I became fascinated with the consistency of the findings. It seemed that regardless of whether the researchers whose papers I was reading worked with winning volleyball teams, successful executives, pilots who made it through flight training, children who succeeded in school, or any other variety of "winner," the profile of traits in each of these categories of people was very similar. After months of studying these many research reports, I concluded that a "Success Factor" (or "S-Factor") did, indeed, exist.

The next task before me was to examine clinical material, case histories as well as research reports, to determine whether there was good evidence of cross-discipline success. If there is such a thing as an S-Factor, and you have it, shouldn't you be able to succeed at anything you try? Once more, this study was encouraging. Every major study as well as my own clinical experience shows this to be true. If you have the S-Factor you can win at anything—almost!

Last, I traced many case histories to determine whether this S-Factor was hereditary or could be acquired through learning. On this there are mixed opinions. Certainly, it helps to be born with a whopping I.Q. But, we all know many people who are extremely successful without benefit of particularly high intelligence. How do they do it? Is it possible that the S-Factor is not directly related to intelligence? My studies show this to be true too. The S-Factor is a combination of traits enabling you to use the intelligence and personality you have, and does not depend on how much of either you were blessed with from birth.

In general, the S-Factor seems to have the following attributes:

1. It is a series of qualities encompassing how you feel about being successful as well as how others react to you—whether you are perceived by others as a winner.
2. It isn't just one quality but a collection that scientists like to call a "profile."
3. If you have the S-Factor, you are likely to succeed at anything you try.
4. You have a head start if you were born a genius but those of us who weren't shouldn't despair. S-Factor people are also of average intelligence.
5. Finally, if you know what the S-Factor traits are, you can shape your own personality to conform more nearly to it, ensuring you will get the most out of what you have.

"S OR NO?" THAT IS THE QUESTION

Why, one may ask, did a perfectly happy psychiatrist set off on a quest for the S-Factor and decide to write a book about his findings? Furthermore, who might read such a book? The first answer is that success is here to stay and most of us want to be a part of it.

It's also nice to have a winner for a spouse and, in business, it comes in handy to work with winners, whether you're the boss hiring a new employee or an employee wondering whether you should invest the next ten years of your career in the hands of the bald man with the wrinkled grey pinstripe suit who just offered you a job.

We want to have successful children, we crave it for ourselves. It's important to know precisely, in each instance, just how likely you are to have a successful spouse, boss, child or self and, if not, what you can do to help bring this about.

Yet, most of us act on instinct alone. Even though the most important decisions of our lives concern who we marry, for whom we work, how we raise our children and how we develop ourselves, we rely on gut feelings alone in this realm. We stubbornly insist on superimposing our dreams and expectations on the world rather than trying to shape the world from what is already there and possible.

"Not true," you say? Well, see if Karen and Jim's case sounds familiar.

When Karen got pregnant, she and Jim were overjoyed. They had long anticipated starting a family and had worked out exactly how to balance her career with having a baby. She and Jim had spent lots of time making preparations for the new arrival. They took Lamaze classes together. They bought a two-bedroom condo when they made plans to have a baby and fixed up the "baby's" room together. They even fantasized about which colleges their child would attend in later years: Brown, Karen's alma mater, if a girl. Colgate, if a son, just like his father.

The baby boy arrived to eagerly waiting parents but joy soon turned into concern. The child had a congenital malformation called spina bifida. This is a condition in which the spinal cord and its covering are laid open near their base, causing weakness or paralysis of the lower limbs and requiring close care throughout life to minimize other possible complications. Jim and Karen were good and dedicated parents for their son. They were also extremely disappointed but failed to acknowledge this feeling. Inwardly, each of them retained the image of the child expected but not received and both of them felt a continuing loss. Jim, upset that Mark would never play baseball like he did as a boy, or might never ride a bicycle or even roller-skate, was blinded to what his son could do. Karen felt similar disappointment and avoided recognizing Mark's potential as well. Both parents overlooked the fact that the child had extraordinary intelligence and musical talent. They pictured a son with a baseball bat in his hand standing at home plate, not a boy with a violin and bow in his hands, sitting in a wheelchair.

So when Mark came home from school and told them he wanted to enroll in the after-school orchestra program, they nodded automatic assent without paying much attention. After a year passed, they attended the school orchestra recital. They were surprised to find that Mark was the soloist and was phenomenal, even after only one year of so-so instruction. They decided to get behind his musical career and push as hard as they could, feeling that they had now uncovered a quality in him that would "get him going in life."

Mark was enrolled in a conservatory and made spectacular progress. It was a shock to them when his violin teacher called and asked to speak with them about his depression.

"Depressed?" Karen repeated with surprise and indignation. "Mark's never been happier since he found himself through music."

Mr. Sirota, his violin teacher, answered, "Yes, the violin has been a breakthrough for Mark. But he's depressed. I have come to know this boy and to love his spirit. He's starved for affection—always seeking to please, dying for a grain of approval."

"Wait a minute," Jim shot back. "You're making Mark sound like some sort of neurotic. He's got problems. Any kid who grew up in a wheelchair would. But he's not the wilting flower you're describing."

Mr. Sirota offered them a note to read, written in Mark's handwriting. It brought tears to their eyes. It said:

"Dear Mr. Sirota. I wonder if there is a school somewhere where children could live and study violin. I never meet any kids like me. I have no friends. Maybe if I went to such a school I wouldn't be so lonely. Please don't tell my parents I asked you for this. Make it sound like it was your suggestion. I also would like you to hurry. Thanks a lot. (signed) Mark"

"We don't really know our boy," Karen said, sobbing through her handkerchief. Jim's eyes were red and tear-filled.

"He's our son—sensitive, talented and lonely," Jim said. "He's not aggressive, like what we expected a son of ours to be. And he can't walk." While they knew that all the time, Karen and Jim never really faced the impact that reality had on Mark. They were too consumed with their own disappointment to recognize Mark's needs. They needed to get to know their son and to acknowledge what he was and not what they had hoped he would be.

Whether you're concerned with the success of your child, your spouse or yourself, if you don't know what's inside a person, you won't know how to foster success. It's as simple as that. There may be a gold mine there just waiting to be discovered. Yet, if you come looking for oil, you'll never find the gold that's there.

That reminds me of a day I spent with my friend, Walter, the owner of a successful service company. He was showing me around his company and crying the blues about his help. "They're a bunch of boobs. Nobody has ambition any more. It's not like in the early days when people were hungry and would put out a decent day's work for a fair day's pay. Now, their attitude is 'gimme.' I tell you, if I have another lousy fiscal quarter, I'll sell the damned place and retire."

"Maybe people haven't changed but you have," I challenged Walt.

"How so?" he queried.

"Well, in the early days, you were hungry yourself and looking for talent in people that could help you build an empire. You were willing to overlook their flaws as long as they could be useful to you. Now you've grown prosperous and spoiled. You aren't looking for gold in people. It's more important to you now if someone's flaws irritate you than if their contributions enrich you."

Walt frowned, then gave me a friendly punch on the shoulder and said, "You're right you son-of-a-gun, but I hate to admit it."

Can You Deliver The Goods?

You may want to shine in life or polish someone else's talent. But first you must know what to look for and how and where to search. Not every attribute you associate with success is necessarily important. Many attributes you would have overlooked are important. Take the following test and see how closely your profile matches that of a person who has the S-Factor.

Answer True or False to the Following Questions:

T   F

1. I believe that being organized stifles creativity and success.
2. Most of the obstacles to success come from lack of the right breaks or not having the right connections.
3. I am a winner.

T   F

4. Stubborn people often get lost in blind alleys on the way to success.
5. I think I'm quite special.
6. I often imagine what it would be like to be in another career or to live someone else's life.
7. I take advantage of opportunities.
8. I like being accepted.
9. I'm considered to be very generous.
10. I can close my eyes right now for a few minutes and concentrate on what I have just read in this chapter without being distracted by my inner thoughts and feelings.

If you answered every question correctly, close the book and spend your time relaxing. You deserve a rest. Most likely, you've already achieved much success in your life.

If you had even one mistake, there is an element lacking in your personality with regard to how you strive for success, one crucial gap that may hamper all your best efforts.

In future chapters, I will go over the attributes covered by this test and help you to understand their significance, how to test for them and acquire them or promote them in others. For, clearly, the S-Factor is not one quality alone. Since it describes the total personality of a successful person, it is a complex alloy of many individual qualities. These are:

1. *Rigidity*. The successful person seems to be on the rigid side but not to an extreme. Mostly, the rigidity reflects itself in a stubborn adherence to a self-concept as a winner. The rigidity also comes through in the deliberate rather than swashbuckling manner by which tasks are attacked. (See Chapter 2)
2. *Organization*. The successful individual is focused, difficult to distract and is concerned with controlling as many factors as possible that affect his or her life and work. This begins, primarily, with self-control.
3. *Self-Esteem*. The successful individual has a great deal of pride either arising from a childhood experience with credible and interested parents who gave credible praise; or an adulthood in which persistent reliance on the self has resulted in a strong self-concept.

4. *Creativity and Tough-Mindedness.* The successful person is able to conceptualize and attack problems in novel ways and does so in a persistent manner until the problem has been solved.
5. *Introversion/Extroversion.* Depending on whether the person succeeds in individual or group exploits, he or she is introverted or extroverted, respectively.
6. *Physical Health.*
7. *Intelligence.* Rather than having a significantly higher level of intelligence than most, the person with the S-Factor has a very practical and useful approach to learning. He or she is the best implementer rather than the quickest learner in the crowd.

The combination of traits listed above is bound to include some that every individual lacks. Use the workshop section (Part II of this book) to assess which ones you might be missing and strengthen your capacities in those.

ANSWERS

1. F
2. F
3. T
4. F
5. T
6. T
7. T
8. F
9. F
10. T

2
HERE COMES THE JUDGE
Rigidity and Self-Punishment

This guy's a plodder. He's very deliberate, not loose and spontaneous. He's a rigid person who has an intolerance for distractions. Under stress, he stubbornly maintains he is O.K. rather than looking at himself and questioning his own abilities in order to improve the way he operates.

Is this the guy you always thought of as a winner? I'll bet not!

Odds are you thought the personality described above is more likely associated with soldiers rather than generals. Yet, surprisingly, generals, if they are winners, would be exactly like the person described above. That's one of the confounding things you will discover when you study successful people. They often look anything but successful. Yet scientific studies show that people who are successful have some very surprising traits.

Take the fellow described above. Is a successful person rigid, plodding, controlling? Does he or she have tunnel vision? On some occasions, that's exactly what successful people have in common—and for some very good reasons, when you analyze the facts.

Let's examine the psychological profile of Andrew, a senior

vice president of a multinational corporation. There is no question about his current level of success. He has made it to the top of one of the world's largest and most successful corporations. He is envied by colleagues and subordinates alike. A close confidant of the chairman of the corporation, he is consulted on every major corporate decision. The chairman wouldn't make a move unless Andy "signed off" on it. You would like Andy if you met him. Except for one trait—he's a bit too controlling and rigid. He takes a long time to make a decision and goes about his work very methodically.

At lunch one day, I asked Andy if he had ever had a psychological profile done on himself. He said yes and was kind enough to furnish me with a psychological profile done twenty-nine years earlier when he was being considered for his first job in the company. Studying his personality profile yielded some interesting surprises.

He was clearly of superior intelligence. That added up. What didn't compute was the fact that he scored only "average" on indicators measuring leadership skills and insight and just above average on human relations skills. Surprising, too, was his score on rigidity. He turned out to be a person who didn't freewheel. Rather, he made deliberate plans for everything he did and stuck to them assiduously. What we had, way back then, was a young man who didn't look like he might turn out to be a great leader. He didn't have the charisma and free spirit of the stereotypical entrepreneur. He looked much more like a follower, a good soldier, than a general. Yet, twenty-nine years later, time proved him to be an exceptional leader and a huge success.

Why are "rigidity" and "being deliberate" so important for success? Let's look at a piece of research to understand why a rigid person might have an advantage over anyone else, when it comes to success.

In a study of students in high school and college who scored in the superior range academically, it was found that these high performers had quite rigid personalities. Further analysis showed why.

Facing stress, a rigid person tends to have an inflexible self-concept. It is as if he or she thinks, "I'm a winner. Just because

I'm staring failure in the face, it doesn't change anything. If I plod ahead persistently, I will surely be able to vindicate my belief in myself."

By contrast, bright students who are not as rigid when facing stress begin to doubt their own capacities. They say, "Am I really as capable as I think? After all, there have been times when I screwed up. Maybe this will be one of them."

The more "flexible" student is apt to change his or her self-concept under stress whereas the bullheaded, rigid one will just continue on as if nothing could ever dent his or her self-confidence. The flexible student is more "correct" to use insight and reflect upon the potential for failure as well as the possibility of success. The rigid student is less insightful for ignoring the possibility of failure. But, consistently, it appears that a person who can ignore the possibility of failure under stress will succeed more often!

A study of professional women golfers separated the athletes into two groups: the champions and the rest of the pros. They were given psychological tests wherein it was found that the champions were more rigid as well as more confident. Maybe this says something about the roots of self-confidence. Perhaps it's not enough to believe in yourself. Maybe you have to be single-minded and stubborn about that belief, even when events suggest you might fail or actually have failed.

If you are rigid, you say, "What the hell, I'll succeed next time out." If you're more reasonable and insightful, you might recognize the possibility of failure and resign yourself to that fate. Either way, it appears that a self-fulfilling prophecy occurs. If you can't conceive of yourself as a failure, you don't fail. If you can see yourself failing, more often you do. Better to be rigid about your self-appraisal than reasonable—at least if you want to be a champion.

Champions don't get off too easily emotionally. They occasionally do fail and when they do, they are brutally self-critical, as if failure was a demon that simply can't exist in their lives and must be exorcised immediately. You don't believe me? Ever watch John McEnroe on a tennis court after he misses an easy return? There is an exorcism ritual if I ever saw one! The champion punishes himself after failure, not for failing, but for being stupid enough to let himself fail when he knows he's a champion and didn't have to lose.

The personality traits of rigidity, self-punitiveness and the predisposition for being highly organized and regimented sound awfully close to what we might diagnose as an obsessive-compulsive neurotic. Is there a link between this condition and winning? The research of the last ten years suggests that there is.

A study of college students attempted to determine which ones might fare better on ambiguous tasks. It is well known that to be successful you often have to persevere in a situation that doesn't yield a clear answer or way out. Winners must often stare a muddled situation in the face and continue on until they find a solution after people of lesser tenacity have quit and accepted failure.

In one study of college students, the entire group was given a series of very ambiguous tasks. Then, personality tests were administered. The interesting result was that the two groups scoring highest on the solution of ambiguous tasks were people who scored highest on either neurotic or self-actualizing personality traits. This reinforces a myth that probably has some truth to it, that being a little crazy is often an ingredient in the personality of successful people.

People often are afraid to enter psychotherapy because they fear the psychiatrist may induce a cure of a neurotic trait they hold responsible for both their pain as well as for their success. The studies of successful people partially bear this out—if you want to succeed, you have to be somewhat obsessive-compulsive. But it is a matter of degree. It pays to be somewhat obsessive-compulsive about one's work. However, at an extreme, this condition is paralytic and ensures failure.

Let's look at the mental organization that operates in the condition we call the obsessive-compulsive neurosis.

We all have a conscience. As in the story of *Goldilocks and the Three Bears*, in some of us our conscience is too soft, with others it is too harsh and with others it is just right. Some people let themselves off the hook too easily. They can cheat and steal and yet their conscience finds a way to cushion the guilt and let them continue. Other people persecute themselves for the slightest reason. You look at them the wrong way and they wonder, "What did I do wrong to displease you?" They guilt-trip themselves into atoning for their "bad behavior" and, at first, it makes them work harder and more effectively. At another level of self-punitiveness, they become paralyzed and ineffectual. Then there are people for whom the conscience is like a good friend—telling them what they need to hear about themselves and their flaws but being supportive and encouraging as well. For these people, self-criticism sounds like this: "I know I messed up. I can do better next time and I will because I'm basically a good person."

Winners come from the latter two groups: those with slightly too harsh a conscience and those with a balanced conscience. People with a balanced conscience are winners who live happy lives, comfortable in their personalities and with their successes. However, people with harsh consciences can also be winners. The person who is highly self-punitive may have developed a way to cope with that disposition. He might make a pact with himself that, in order to prevent further expression of his defects, he must be highly organized, regimented, planful, rigidly hard-working and inflexible about his principles. Such a person has the characteristics found in high-achieving students, championship tennis players and in Andrew, the senior vice president of the multinational who made it to the top without great leadership or interpersonal skills.

There is an exception to the rule that winners are rigid and very deliberate. A study conducted by the famous British behavioral scientist, Dr. Eysenck, showed that if you look at artists who have been rated as being successful by experts in their given field of art, the ones who are at the top consistently come out higher on "psychoticism" traits than all the rest.

Art is a field in which, in order to be successful, you must break the rules and take a different view of reality than those around you. Hence, great artists have psyches that are closer to those of psychotics who break from reality than to obsessive-compulsive neurotics who win within the confines of rules and regulations. So if you want to be a successful artist, tell your psychiatrist to leave some of your idiosyncratic thinking alone. Whereas if you want to be a success most everywhere else, tell your shrink not to cure you of all your guilts and compulsive hang-ups. That little conscience that sits inside, judging our behavior and ordering us to atone for our sins through hard work and discipline, is also what makes us win in situations where others of more balanced sanity will "see the writing on the wall," cut their losses and quit in a "hopeless" situation. It's time the conscience, our internal "judge," got more respect.

If you want to know whether your internal "judge" is too harsh, or just tough enough on you to propel you to the top, take the "Here Comes The Judge" test that follows:

T   F

1. When I make a mistake, I know everyone notices it.
2. The last time I made a mistake, I couldn't get over it for days. It still bothers me.
3. It doesn't pay to dwell on your errors. You're much better off going on to the next challenge.
4. Most of my failures have been due to bad luck or the interference of others.
5. I have succeeded in some important things by luck alone.
6. I know that some day others will discover many of my inadequacies.
7. I feel so much guilt about certain things I have done that no amount of repentance seems to relieve the guilt feelings.

Scoring

Give yourself one point for every true answer. If you scored 0-1, you have a reasonable conscience. A score of 2-3 indicates you have neurotic guilt: enough to make you uncomfortable and probably enough also to motivate you toward success. A score of 4-7 indicates a crippling level of guilt that clearly needs professional help.

Remember, there is a difference between guilt and rigidity when it comes to success. Guilt inhibits. Rigidity enhances endurance.

Guilt, the internal judge, can be a strong ally and friend for the emotionally healthy, a tormentor and provocateur for the neurotically successful, or a prison warden for the guilt-ridden who are immobilized in failure.

If you want to reduce your level of neurotic guilt, try the following:

Imagine that your self-criticism is being uttered by a third party. Look over at an empty chair in the same room where you are now seated. Imagine a person sitting in that chair saying to you what your internal judge says about you inside. For example, if after you commit an error, you like to rush on to the next challenge, it is likely that you are doing this under the influence of an internal judge (your conscience) that says, "Shame on you, you turkey. You did it again, you boob. You're always screwing up." Under this kind of internal goading, you are likely to want to just get the hell out of there and go on to the next challenge. The problem is, you don't pause long enough to learn how to correct your current mistake. You flee in disgrace, shamed by a too harsh conscience.

Now, imagine that a person sitting in that empty chair has just said to you what your internal judge said to you. How would you feel being called a "turkey" and "boob" by someone sitting over there? I'll bet you'd be furious. You'd feel like punching him, right?

Well, if you want to, you can get rid of that guy in the chair and the one in your head as well. It's up to you. You put them both there and can kick them out any time you want. The problem is, we forget we have the power over our own conscience. We think it is the reverse—that it rules us.

The next time your mind says once too often, "Here comes the judge," you can decide, "There goes that judge...out of my life, once and for all!"

3

THE INTERNAL COMPASS
Organization

What's your image of the successful American entrepreneur? Mine is a man or woman sitting at the head of a mahogany boardroom table, staring down the length of its gleaming surface at reports prepared by subordinates to whom the "boss" has delegated all the important tasks of the organization. The big cheese is surrounded by the rest of the crackers in my view of a classic American success story.

My fantasy successful entrepreneur in the elegant boardroom may operate in real life as I've imagined, but that's not necessarily the image the successful entrepreneur has of him- or herself.

There's a real difference between top executive behavior and privately held attitude. Inside the grey-pinstriped mind of the team-playing, successful entrepreneur is a masked man, riding alone on his horse in any direction he chooses. His entire entourage of subordinates represent no more to him than did Tonto to the Lone Ranger—comforting to know he's there and occasionally good to have in a pinch, but not someone from whom to take advice and direction.

The successful entrepreneur is a loner of the first order, seeking goals of his or her own choosing and looking internally for resources with which to control his or her destiny. One characteristic of successful people from all walks of life is their internal accountability—they see themselves as responsible for gaining the success they seek and look inside for the strengths with which to achieve it.

While I have personally interviewed many hundreds of successful executives and celebrities and have found this trait in virtually all of them, I decided to search the scientific literature to see if this trait held true in other arenas of success. I found it did, and with startling regularity.

In the group of professional women golfers surveyed, the champions of the group were found to reflect strongly the attitude of internal accountability.

In scientific circles, this is called an internal locus of control. These champion women golfers differed from other professional competitors in the degree to which they held themselves accountable for their successes and failures.

Champions never really blame another person for failure, even though they may appear to from time to time. Inside, a fire burns in the conscience when failure is encountered and it rages until it consumes every iota of blame. The real champion emerges from this process, cleansed by an internal anger that sweeps away all alibis for failure and reinforced by a successful search for internal resources with which to compete all the more fiercely the next time.

A survey of highly successful working women showed that those at the top had a strong internal locus of control, just as do champion women golfers. What about other groups? Does this rule hold true for them too?

Psychology graduate students whose careers were tracked in later years showed that those with a strong internal locus of control were the ones who ended up with the most professional success. A national survey of people from all walks of life, which traced people's progress from age fifteen to age thirty, showed the same thing—hold yourself responsible for success and failure and you will reap success. Blame others and you will end up an "also ran."

Perhaps the most significant of all examples illustrating the value of having a high internal locus of control is a study of disadvantaged children who had made good in later years. In case after case, those children who were able successfully to overcome the disadvantages of poverty, racism and a welfare mentality were those who were able to hold themselves responsible for their emancipation. Through the shaping of their personalities by parents and teachers, these children grew up with a strong conviction that, in order to get out of the ghetto, they would have to learn to initiate and pursue independent courses of action that differed from the influences and experiences around them. One such case was that of Thomas.

In the New Haven inner-city ghetto where he grew up, it was a predictable course of events to go to school without much interest, viewing education as an unnecessary and boring delay on the road to welfare, drugs and, perhaps, a year or more in legal detention. The local elementary school was viewed as the "white man's institution," even though many of the teachers were black and the student body was overwhelmingly black. Conceiving of the school as "not ours," many black parents and their children developed antagonistic attitudes towards education, linking it with other aspects of their oppression. Not so Thomas's mother.

Elva was a single parent with very limited educational background, never having finished elementary school herself. She worked as a housekeeper and raised her three children herself, recruiting each of them into sharing responsibilities as soon as they were able. Elva had no time or patience for self-pity. Less even for blame. "I don't see no white people stopping you from learning your math," she chided her son, Thomas, when he was caught cheating on a math test. He tried to blame his teacher, a white woman, for not caring about black kids. Elva was unimpressed. "I attend every parent-teachers meeting," she hollered. "I'm on a committee to study new ways of getting parents and children to participate in the running of the school. Don't go telling me that this school doesn't care for black children, Thomas. Black kids are the school."

"Whatsamatter, Mom," Thomas needled, "they gonna give you a diploma or something for acting like an Oreo Cookie?"

As he said this he started to run, knowing that his mother would be after him in moments with a belt, stick or frying pan.

Throughout his youth, Elva relentlessly hammered home the idea that this was his school, not the property of the white establishment. She proved this with her own actions by participating constructively rather than criticizing the institution as if she were an outsider. Eventually Thomas was influenced by her attitude and began to participate in rather than oppose the school. Elva's self-sufficiency rubbed off on her son. Her strong internal locus of control allowed her to go against the grain of the attitudes held by many parents in the community who preferred to attack the school rather than assist it. Thomas learned from her example to carve an independent pathway for himself. Strengthened by a firm internal locus of control, he was able to resist the taunts of his peers who felt he, too, was becoming an Oreo for his increasing interest in academics, particularly science and math. Thomas spent less and less time on street corners and more in the community library. Eventually, he was admitted to a highly ranked university and was launched on a permanent trajectory to success. Elva's example was the fuel that boosted him out of the ghetto. The internal locus of control he developed was his guidance system. Going against the grain, led only by your own dreams and ambitions, is what makes winners.

Take the following test to assess the strength of your internal guidance system for success:

Answer the following questions by indicating the strength of your belief from one to five: one being almost never true; two seldom true; three true half the time; four frequently true; five almost always true.

1 2 3 4 5

1. When I don't know the answer to a problem, I look for a resource book or expert to show me the correct solution.
2. I like to celebrate Christmas the same way each year.
3. Heights make me nervous.
4. Give kids freedom and they'll use it to find trouble.

1 2 3 4 5

5. Government can't be responsive to people's needs.
6. I have read the owner's manual for almost every piece of equipment I own.
7. If you pay attention to someone's gripes, they tend to complain more.

Scoring and Interpretation

Questions one and six: give yourself minus one to five for the answers as you scored them.

Questions 2,3, 4, 5 and 7, give yourself plus one to five for the answers as you scored them.

Tally up the scores for all questions. The LOWER the final score, the STRONGER your internal locus of control.

Scores range from minus five to plus twenty-three.

1. In question one, if you search for answers from an expert source, you are still taking responsibility for the search. What should you do when you don't know the solution and have tried to figure it out for yourself without success? Wait for divine intervention?
2. If you like repeating any experience the same way from year to year, you are a traditionalist. There's nothing wrong with that. However, it also reflects a reliance on external structure rather than on internal direction.
3. People who are afraid of heights doubt their own ability to control their impulses, a sure sign of a weak internal locus of control.
4. In this question, if you feel that most often freedom is dangerous, you will not crave much for yourself or use it well.
5. Government may not always be responsive to people, but it can be if we make legislators accountable to us. Someone with a weak internal locus of control would give up and conclude it's a lost cause.
6. If you own a piece of equipment and haven't read the owner's manual, you are the type who expects things not to go wrong or, when they do, you look to someone else to fix it. Those with a strong internal locus of control want the expertise in their grasp as soon and as firmly as

possible.

7. If you have no patience for another person's gripes and feel that complaints encourage complaining, you probably are guilty of the same thing you can't tolerate in others—blaming someone else for your own problems.

"The buck stops here," was a sign that didn't end up on a president's desk by accident. Champions and leaders are internally directed. That doesn't mean they aren't open to the opinions of others or sensitive to the influences around them. However, it does mean that, after all is said and done, the winner will emerge from the pack as the person who has the best grasp of how he or she can improve, apply and direct inner resources towards the tasks to be accomplished.

4
FROM PRIDE TO PERFORMANCE
Self-Esteem

Are you afraid that your job will be taken over one day by a computer possessed of more artificial intelligence than you have of the real thing? I'm not. At least, not after having researched the relationship between pride and performance.

The vast preponderance of the literature suggests that having the skills to win is not enough to make you come out on top. The winning edge is good, old-fashioned pride. I'm quite sure that no matter how much RAM, ROM or elegant code you feed a computer, it will never develop pride in what it is and does. Let's look at the role of pride in achieving success.

In one study, behavioral scientists looked at the relationship between self-esteem (their term for pride) and two critical success predictors: (1) desire for success and (2) expectation of success. They found that consistent winners always had both a desire and an expectation of success while the less successful may have high desire but not high expectations. Along with both high desire and high expectation came high self-esteem (or maybe the latter creates the former two). Let's look at these components of success more deeply.

To win in sports you have to have a great deal of desire. This has been borne out over the years since a Notre Dame football team was infused with desire by the immortal phrase, "Win one for the Gipper." Coaches know that to get top performance from a team they must keep the team's desire at a high level. But they fear their team becoming overconfident, thus losing desire and giving the other team the psychological advantage of being the underdog. A sports team must be confident and not complacent.

A burning desire to win comes from the feeling that the team's honor is at stake and that it must earn the victory over a worthy adversary in order to vindicate its pride and uphold its reputation. Victory over a pushover would tarnish rather than enhance team pride. In other words, desire is fed from within by a sense of personal pride and from without by a feeling that the cause is worth fighting for and the adversary is a worthy opponent.

Pride has yet another component. The proud competitor expects to win at all times. From the top of his backswing right down to the wing tips of his golf shoes, the competitor with high self-esteem believes him- or herself to be a winner. Going out on a sales call, the person with pride expects to close every sale, even though, at some other level of logic, there is a recognition that this rate of success is impossible. Pride powers the successful competitor to ignore the odds and go for a win every time out.

That's the stuff that the New York Yankee dynasty years were made of. That's what propels I.B.M. to continuously dominate the office automation field. From this relentless expectation to win, the space program drew the persistence that allowed it to overtake the Russians and be the first to put a man on the moon—only decades after man first learned to fly.

If there is a psychological definition for the "Right Stuff," it is self-esteem with its two-fisted attributes of intense desire and an irrational expectation to win all the time.

Pride, or self-esteem, is a key factor in achieving occupational success as well. Let's look at a scientific study of the typical American success story, the immigrant who comes to this country without anything and makes good.

In a study of immigrant families, particular attention was

paid to the achievement of the children of these naturalized Americans. Several factors came out of this study which accounted for the fact that certain families produced exceptional high rates of achievement in their children. Quality of primary schooling was an expected finding in those high-achieving families as was quality of home accommodations. After all, if the environmental circumstances at home and school are superior for the child, we would expect that child to hold an advantage over another one with less nurturing and less-convenient surroundings.

The most significant finding, however, was the one that showed parental interest to be the strongest factor in the later achievement of these first-generation children. What this study revealed goes to the heart of how self-esteem is created in us all.

According to the latest theories of personality development, self-esteem is the central core of the personality. It is the gyroscope of the psyche, keeping it on course through turbulent times and unknown territories.

A person with defects in personal pride or self-esteem will suffer more than the fate of being unsuccessful. Lacking an expectation of success, this person would fold his cards when the going got rough or the terrain looked unfamiliar. Someone with a better sense of self would go on, encouraged by the relentless expectation of success that comes along with high self-esteem.

The person with low self-esteem would also suffer grave self-doubt about many other aspects of life, especially interpersonal relationships, feeling rejection when there is none intended. And when rejected, feeling that he or she has lost everything precious rather than merely being denied someone else's approval of what he or she holds precious. The person with low self-esteem compensates, unsurely but often, with bravado for the feeble sense of self, reinforcing the ego with possessions, mind-altering potions or a thirst for power. Never satisfied, the person with low self-esteem always hungers for more symbols of an accomplished self and is never convinced by their acquisition. Just like someone with high self-esteem, the person with low self-esteem has an intense desire to win but, unlike the former, there is an irrational belief he will lose. No matter how much is accomplished, he never feels secure. No matter how much he is appreciated, he never feels wanted. No matter how much she earns, she never feels satisfied. Eventually, this person, trapped between an intense desire to win and a constant fear of losing all, becomes depleted, depressed and defeated. The most frequent statement made by such people in a psychiatric office is, "Doctor, I have everything I have ever dreamed of and more; yet I'm unhappy and I don't know why."

Take the case of Sam. The child of immigrant parents, his life was rough at the beginning. Both his parents worked, his mother as a seamstress and his father owned a small luncheonette in an industrial building. Sam's days were lonely as a youngster since both parents worked long hours, leaving him at home to fend for himself. That experience guaranteed that, in later life, he would never be at a loss when left on his own. Somehow Sam would always cope in any tough situation. The lessons he had learned as a child served him well throughout his life, leading to his successful career as a stockbroker. He always managed to plug a little harder than the next guy and earn more for his clients who were, of course, highly grateful for his efforts. Yet, Sam never really believed in his success. He was as frightened of it as would be a lion tamer, never knowing at which moment his success might turn on him and devour him.

"I can't even swallow my food at lunchtime," he complained. "I sit in the restaurant, gulping down my lunch, thinking that the minutes I'm spending there might cost me a big client."

I asked Sam, "Even though you know (because clients have told you and stuck with you over the years) that they trust you and believe in your judgment, why is it that you still fear making just one mistake or missing just one opportunity will cause the whole house to topple down around your ears?"

"I don't know why I feel that way but it's killing me. I haven't been able to get a good night's sleep for a long time. I'm into sleeping pills and booze at night, cocaine during the day and still nothing works."

I asked, "What would it take to reassure you that you are safe, that you're not in danger of being robbed of your success or the qualities in you that brought you to that goal?"

"Funny you should say that about 'my qualities' that brought me to success. I never think of it that way. I usually feel I've been lucky to be in the right place at the right time and have more persistence than the next guy. I work harder because I'm at a disadvantage. They know more than I do so I have to struggle harder to make up for that lead." At that point, Sam seemed to get sadder and fell silent.

"Sam," I asked, "do you remember anyone ever telling you that you were special or exceptional?"

His eyes filled with tears and he wiped them away with a stubby-fingered hand weighed down by a thick gold bracelet. "My parents were always at work. Even when my father made money, bought out several restaurants and we could live better than most other people, he still dedicated all his interest to his work and his investments. My mother became preoccupied with being a 'society lady' and didn't give me the time of day either. Money, they gave me plenty. Interest, zero. I always felt I wasn't important at home."

That recognition was the beginning of the long rebuilding process for Sam's self-esteem that ultimately gave him the sense of personal worth and contentment that he had sought for so many years.

Self-esteem requires two crucial ingredients for its development:

1. interest and credible praise
2. interested and credible parents

Of what value is interest and praise given by parents whose own example is inadequate? What impact can parents have on a child if they are good role models but never reflect to the child a sense of pride in his or her accomplishments or interest in his or her life? So crucial to success is the development of a strong sense of self that we must study how it is created in detail. Without a firm grasp of the origins of self-esteem, the remedies and recommendations that could lead you to a more successful life would lack depth and durability.

As we saw in the case of Sam, the crucial center of the process of self-esteem development is the relationship (or lack of it) between empathic parents and the child. The empathic parent operates on two channels at once—one tuned into the self and the other constantly monitoring the child's world. The signals rarely get mixed up. Healthy parents don't feel *like* their children—they feel *for* their children. Sam's parents should have known he needed their interest, not their money. An empathic parent would have been alert to this and delivered what the child needed.

A special relationship evolves between an empathic parent and dependent child. The parent senses not only fears and insecurities in the child but also unused potential, budding initiative and skills struggling through the awkward states towards the mastery level. The empathic parent senses this awakening strength and reinforces it by expressing interest in how the child is applying skills in his or her own world. Praise is given only when it is truly deserved, giving validity to the parent's compliments. When the child sees interest and pride in the parent's eyes, the child feels confident about a personal ability to handle the world. Such a parent knows how hard it is to cope at times and recognizes how valiantly the child is testing skills in lieu of dependency on the parent. Such a parent reassures that help will be available if needed. And most of the time the child is not disappointed. Mom or Dad is there when needed and will lend strength where it is lacking.

Self-esteem develops through this process: empathic parents showing interest in their children and giving credible praise. Having described what you might think is the ideal parent-child relationship, let me contradict myself immediately. If the process went as smoothly as depicted, self-esteem would not develop at all. The child would learn to expect perfect empathy and reassurance and would know that Mom and Dad are always around when they are needed. Hence, why try to be more self-sufficient?

In fact, self-esteem develops best when there are slight failures of empathy—lapses too small to cause scars and just large enough to alert the child to the need to develop personal resources. These parental boo-boos are called "optimal frustrations." They are the saving grace of a child's development and what makes parenting tolerable, even possible. Each time a parental lapse occurs, the child must invent a way to cope on its own. The child isn't happy about this letdown. Rage ensues. The parents mustn't be allowed to get off scot-free for these failures. But, at the same time, the child is forced to make do with his or her own resources and, most of the time, finds these to be adequate to survival. Hence, the child is reluctantly propelled forward and soon enough overcomes its anger at the parents because, after all, they are good enough most of the time.

Empathy cures the growth-promoting rifts that occur from time to time—the small failures that force the child out of the protective womb and create strength where primitive dependency existed. Reconciliations occur because of empathy. These renew the parent-child relationship, but now at a higher level of competency, confidence and self-respect than before. An important sequence is established which will occur in all relationships throughout life:

Empathic bonding
Failure of empathy
Frustration and a need to cope alone
Growth
Expressed resentment
Empathic reconciliation at a more mature level

This sequence of occurrences, repeated many times throughout the life cycle, creates a strong, resilient self—one in constant touch with others at ever higher levels of mutual dependency. It was, in part, the discovery of the importance of this developmental sequence that has revolutionized psychoanalytic theory and practice in the past ten years.

A new psychology of complex behavior has emerged called Self Psychology. This new science of personality development emphasizes the necessity for parents (and psychoanalysts) to utilize empathy to promote personality growth and recognizes that we all exist in a world of people upon whom we are dependent for life. Maturation is seen as a progression in the nature of the dependency state—not as a lifetime journey that leads away from dependency.

Let's deal with the latter view of maturation first. In industry, it used to be fashionable to be viewed as a tough, self-sufficient manager—some even used the term a "KITA" manager (which stood for "Kick-In-The-Ass" manager). The concept was that you could only get ahead if you knew how to keep your distance from people, pushing them to greater productivity, and then discarding them when they were no longer useful to the organization.

Recent experience has produced a better model of management. In the wake of the successful Japanese industrial invasion wherein American goods have been trounced in the marketplace by Japanese products of higher quality and lower price, we have come to realize that traditional values held by the Japanese have been the main difference between their success and our failure. Japanese industrial policy expressed through its managers fosters employee identification with the organization, not with the union which sits as an adversary to the organization.

Following this Japanese example, top management in this country has begun to recognize and promote managers who can win the loyalty and support of a "stable" of subordinates. Terms such as the "quality of work life" and "quality circles" suddenly have become popular in the U.S.A. This industrial awakening has paralleled the discovery, on the psychoanalytic front, that while we mature, we never outgrow the need for others. We are only complete when our relationships with others complement the core aspects of the self. No manager is successful without an alliance with peers and subordinates. No person is complete without a cadre of friends who complement his or her core personality attributes. And no child can develop to healthy maturity without learning how to develop such a set of self-completing relationships.

Interdependency is crucial for success. Having a strong self-esteem makes it possible for people to bond to one another without becoming overly dependent and passive or fleeing into isolation out of a fear of being dominated.

Let's look at some "real world" research data for a moment to see how the role of self-esteem operates in performance in various fields.

A study of successful gymnasts showed that the three most important predictors of success were, in order: the coach's expectations; the athlete's own expectations; and the gymnast's past record of achievement. This is an exact parallel of the parent-child situation in which a parent's interest and expectations of the child are vital to the development of self-esteem. A similar study was done on military combat command trainees. Here too, the trainer's expectations were a strong predictor of future success of the trainee.

These and other studies have led behavioral scientists to coin the term "The Pygmalion Effect" to describe the phenomenon by which a nurturing, positive-thinking, encouraging teacher transmits a sense of optimism and high motivation to a student, boosting future performance. The engine of performance is supercharged by self-esteem which, in turn, is fueled by parental (or parent-surrogate) interest.

A converse phenomenon has also been described called, "The Golem Effect," the sad outcome of parental neglect. Here, low parental expectation leads to low performance in a talented or gifted child.

How many of us have experienced both of these phenomena? I think many. We all have felt the sting of rejection and neglect by someone important to us and know how it sucks the wind out of our enthusiasm. We have all felt the sure, encouraging hand of a good teacher or boss that guides us. We know how easy it is, under the mentorship of such a person, to risk striving for a higher level of performance, knowing that a failure will be gently removed from our shoulders by a word of praise and competent guidance. We know that our belief in the mentor and his belief in us will inevitably lead to success.

You might ask, "What about pure luck? Doesn't it have a role to play in achieving success?" The answer is yes, but even here, self-esteem makes us use our luck more effectively. One study showed that if you compared groups of people with high and low self-esteem who had runs of good and bad luck, the ones with low self-esteem would be willing to keep going only as long as they could attribute their success to luck alone. If they failed even once, feeling that luck had deserted them, they would quit rather than rely on their own internal resources.

By contrast, a group of people with high self-esteem who had a run of good luck followed by bad luck wouldn't quit at all. They were more than happy to ride the crest of the wave of good fortune while it lasted, but when luck ran out, self-esteem stayed behind to encourage them to go on until they reached their goal.

In study after study, in every field of endeavor, from business to professional sports, to teaching, to military service, to numerous others, self-esteem came through as the most essential backbone of success. If there is an S-Factor, it stands for self-esteem as much as it does for success.

One last important and fascinating note. A study of seriously ill patients suffering from rheumatoid arthritis showed that those with high self-esteem overcame their handicap far better than patients with low self-esteem. The now famous experience of Norman Cousins showed that illness itself can be overcome by a positive attitude.

It seems that we might now be able to postulate two sets of opposing, natural, mind-body forces of vital importance to health, emotional well-being and success. On the one side is stress, the wear-and-tear factor. On the other side is self-esteem, the source of hope and renewal.

Both these forces seem to operate not only in the mind sphere but also in the biological realm. Stress eventually depletes both physical and emotional strength. Self-esteem endows mind, body and spirit with reservoirs of stamina and hope from which we draw when success seems most remote and with which we make the impossible happen.

5
TOUGH MIND, THICK WALLET

One consistent characteristic of a winner is an attribute known as "tough-mindedness." Nobody doubts that champions have to have guts, be persistent and brave. But somehow, in the culture of quick-drawing cowboy heros, war movies and the ritual Sunday football wars, our concept of what that toughness really means went astray.

We mistake violence for tough-mindedness. We revere recklessness, as long as it is done with dash, never holding it up to the light to notice the absence of thoughtfulness, strategy or even cunning. In the era of the "blitz" and the "quarterback sack," we have downgraded the importance of being able to stick to the game plan.

Winners never make this mistake.

A tough-minded winner isn't brash, showy or even visibly brave. He or she has a more subtle variety of guts which may appear quite different from what you would expect. In the following stories, let's see if you can identify the kind of tough-mindedness found in champions. In each story, there will be two characters exhibiting different reactions to the same situation. Let's see if you can pick the tough-minded one whose thinking pattern is more like that of a champion.

A) Jim and Ed were walking home from the bowling alley on a rainy Friday night. They were tired but satisfied, their team having won the fall tournament. As they rounded a street corner, one block from where they lived, they could see in the distance a small group of about four people gathered. Ed noticed that some of the people were arguing angrily, giving the appearance of some sort of fight just on the threshold of eruption.

Jim, a black belt in karate, turned to Ed and said, "We should probably get out of here before they notice us." Ed, a Golden Glove light heavyweight champion, frowned and replied, "That's just a group of young punks. They have no beef with us. Besides, the two of us could surely polish them off with one hand tied behind our back."

Jim said, "I'd rather not get mixed up in it, just the same. Let's go home the long way round."

Ed said, "Chicken or something?"

Just then, one gang member turned and noticed Jim and Ed standing there and shouted, "Hey, there's a couple of geeks. Lets go after them." And at that moment, the four youths turned and ran towards Ed and Jim.

Ed said, "Jim, are you with me?"

Jim replied, "I'm no damned hero. Let's get the hell out of here."

Analysis

Which of the two would you say was tough-minded in the tradition of a true champion? Ed was ready to stand his ground and bravely resist being pushed around by the young toughs, especially in his own neighborhood. Jim was not prepared to do battle. Who was the tough-minded one?

The literature on winning says Jim was the more tough-minded. It was Jim who, in the face of the challenge and potential threat, was able to assess all the factors. True, both he and Ed were competent at self-defense. And, this was their neighborhood so it would not be a great idea to be known as a coward. That would invite more attacks. But Jim also realized that he and Ed were tired after a night of bowling. Although they could probably have won a fight against all four gang members under ideal circumstances, what about under these conditions? Also, what if one or more of the toughs was carrying a concealed weapon? Jim processed this data quickly and concluded it was smarter to run. It was a tougher decision to turn away from the challenge than to be guided by simple macho pride and stay and fight.

General Douglas MacArthur, in my opinion the greatest military mind of our age, abandoned the field at Corregidor in the face of superior Japanese forces, only to return later in victory and vindication. Tough-mindedness requires digging for guts that the other person didn't know existed. It takes great bravery to admit a potential for loss and accept a loss of face in order to be able to win in the long run.

B) Betty was new on the job at the department store. Mr. Callahan, her boss, a salty old veteran of twenty years in the business, gave her some advice on her first day at work. "You play the game my way here and you'll be all right. Cross me and I'll see to it that you get a pink slip before you know what happened. Understand?"

Shocked and confused, Betty nodded her assent. Callahan figured he had her where he wanted her. Thus began a series of demands and harassments that made going to work a nightmare.

Ellen, a coworker, was sympathetic. "Betty," she advised, "you have to learn how to manipulate this dude. He responds to a little show of femininity. Know what I mean?"

"What do you mean?" Betty replied.

"You're a woman," Ellen chided, "don't tell me you never used your good looks to get something out of a man. Just watch me," she said as she walked over to Mr. Callahan and put her hand suggestively on his shoulder and in a mellifluous and seductive tone of voice asked, "Mr. Callahan, I'm...you know...tired from partying last night. I know I have no right to ask you this, but would you mind it if I left early today?"

Callahan smiled and said, "I'll let you know in a few minutes. Meet me in the coffee room."

Ellen returned to where Betty was standing and said, "Watch this. Come with me to the coffee room and see how I handle this yo-yo."

When they entered the coffee room, they noticed nobody was there. Mr. Callahan came in and said, with a sly grin, "Ellen, I see you're showing Betty the ropes around here." With that, he reached out and touched Betty's buttocks and asked, "Wanna have a drink with me after work?" She recoiled and began to leave the room. Mr. Callahan was enraged. He turned to Ellen and said, "Tell this little bitch what really goes on around here."

Ellen turned and said to Betty, "Let's get the hell out of here."

Callahan warned them as they left the room, "Any trouble out of you two and you're dead ducks."

Ellen and Betty were dumbfounded. Ellen apologized. "The old fart. He never tried to go that far before. He really frightened me. What do you think he'll do?"

Betty replied, "He'll probably try to find an excuse to fire us."

"The bastard," Ellen fumed. "I need this fucking job. I have my daughter to support. If he tries to fire me...just let him try that. I'll have my boyfriend come around tomorrow after closing and speak to him. That bastard Callahan. I'll fix his clock." Betty said, "I wouldn't do that, if I were you. He'd have grounds to fire you then for sure. Maybe he could even get criminal harassment charges against you and your boyfriend."

Ellen replied, scornfully, "What do you propose to do? Give in to him every day to keep him happy?"

"I'm filing a sexual harassment charge against him right away. That ought to stop him."

Ellen laughed, "In this organization, that's like filing a complaint in a casino against losing at blackjack. The place is full of sexual harassment, except they call it, 'The way to get ahead.' Don't be naive, Betty. They'd have you out of here in five minutes if you filed that charge."

Analysis

Ellen felt that "The System" was rigged against women who complained about sexual harassment. She preferred to take the issue up by fighting fire with fire: If Mr. Callahan was going to use threats of firing her to keep her in line, she'd use the threat of her boyfriend beating him up to keep him in line. On her side of the ledger was the fact that, indeed, this organization had a miserable record of enforcing restrictions against sexual harassment. In fact, the corporate culture was more tuned to the exploitation than the protection of women. Hence, Ellen's desire to counter harassment with the threat of violence could be seen as the only rational way out.

Betty, on the other hand, felt that she had a good case for making a charge of sexual harassment stick, in spite of the company's past track record. Mostly, she based this on the fact that there were two women present this time, each able to corroborate the other's allegation of the harassment. Also, she planned to make her charge public, hoping that the other women in the organization, seeing her and Ellen fighting back openly, would come forward and support her charges with experiences of their own.

Betty was right. She won her case against Mr. Callahan and he was fired. Her approach used a persistent intellectual strategy rather than an approach of fighting violence with violence. Betty was assertive. Ellen had planned to be hostile. Research bears out the fact that Betty's assertiveness is much more likely to lead to success.

A study of Air Force cadets showed that the most successful were the least pugnacious by nature. In fact, this group of future military leaders showed the highest level of fear of anybody in their group in dangerous situations. However, their response to fear was not violence or flight but the invocation of intellectual coping mechanisms. In these student officers, fear acted as an early warning signal, giving them a head start in planning an effective response.

Their so-called "brave and fearless" cohorts were far less successful at actually coping when the chips were down because the situations they faced required a deliberate strategic, not an impulsive, pugnacious response. Fear, acting to warn the superior military mind, allowed for time to develop an effective response. The "brave" person tended to minimize the significance of the threat. When the true significance of the threat was finally realized, the "brave" responded in a more impulsive, swashbuckling and less effective manner.

There was a similar finding in a study of student nurses. In this profession where you must see death, mutilation and emergencies daily, the most successful nurses were found to be those who were more task oriented, more tuned into work well done, and less "aggressive." Apparently, strategies of getting the job done are far more useful than guts in medicine.

In my experience in dealing with corporate executives I have found the same to be true. The successful executive is not the one who appears to be the toughest and gutsiest. That's a stereotype best saved for the movies. In real life, the executive who is most likely to succeed is the person who is tough-minded enough to know when to fight and when to flee; when to sue and when not to (even though the case may have merit, it may not be worth winning); and the person who wins is the one who knows how to stick to the task, despite the possibility of failure. Tough-mindedness is not measured by how comfortable you are with hostility but the opposite. It is a trait of high sensitivity to danger which triggers action from a sophisticated intellect that can move swiftly to avoid the danger, even though it may look, on the surface, like cowardice.

The tough-minded executive is a winner who looks like the "guy next door." The future winner is so nondescript that you are never aware that he or she is outsmarting you while you are showing off how tough you are.

6
PEOPLE...WHO NEEDS PEOPLE?

Despite our best efforts to characterize success, to a great extent success is in the eye of the beholder. You may be a success in the eyes of your employees because you are a benevolent boss. On the other hand, your shareholders might think you stink as a corporate leader since your balance sheet isn't what it should be. Still again, the research and development department of your company might be thrilled with you because, although the company isn't as successful as it could be today, it is developing product lines that might propel it to the top of the industry in five years. To make life more complicated, there are your suppliers, your customers, the government regulators and last, but surely not least, your customers to consider.

What do they all think of your success? Can you please them all? Probably not. Hence, if you want to be a success, you must compromise your goals and decide in which arena you wish to succeed, forgoing success in the ones that are incompatible.

Success, when it comes to pleasing other people, is a very varied concept.

Lee Iacocca might have been more successful at Ford Motor

had he been more of an apple polisher. In that case, we might never have seen the Ford Mustang come into existence. He had to choose between being popular with his boss and being effective as a leader. He chose the latter and it cost him his job.

Clearly, we have to adjust our notions of success depending on what goals we wish to achieve and whom we wish to please. One of the most important criteria to consider is whether we wish to have team or individual success since research indicates that the criteria for each are different and often incompatible.

Let's look at the profile of a person who has decided to embark upon a solitary course, be that in business, sports or in life in general. Such an individual would choose a business that doesn't depend upon much interaction with others, or a sport in which individual play is featured. In such cases, a success profile would look as follows:

1.   There would be a low need for nurturance by others. This person would be able to get along for long periods of time without anyone else's approval and could even thrive in the face of disapproval by others. Recall to mind the play of John McEnroe who is becoming a legendary tennis player and, to some, a public nuisance. Were he to need the approval of others in order to succeed, he'd surely be in deep trouble. Nurturance from others is an unnecessary luxury for the solitary champion.

2.   Similarly, solo champions and people who embark upon solitary types of business pursuits are usually not very nurturing to others. One could postulate that there is a chicken and egg phenomenon involved here and that choice of a solo career is caused either by the person's inability to nurture others or that, in order to be successful in a solo career, one has to be more selfish since there is no support from teammates. Either way, the solo winner is not very generous to others, at least not within the context of the professional endeavor.

3.   Research has shown that the solo winner is opportunistic and manipulative. This has been demonstrated in real-life observations and in the behavioral laboratories as

well. A study done of successful salesmen showed that they differed from their less successful compatriots by being less bound by moral principles and more likely to tell people what they want to hear rather than what they believe or what is true. On a personality test, these successful salesmen knew how to fake the results to make themselves look good. In fact, they were able to fake in the direction of personality attributes needed on the job. It seems that the successful salesman is able to construct a false self that gets the job done.

4.　People who succeed in solitary professions have a low level of social awareness. This shows up as a low degree of empathy for others. I suppose in the dog-eat-dog mentality of individual combat, a competitor cannot afford to be too empathic towards others lest he or she lose the desire to annihilate the opponent. In team endeavors, it is easier to appear to be sensitive to others, including one's opponents, because the killer instinct is diluted among the entire team and annihilation is accomplished by committee, a rather less emotionally demanding position.

Examine, for a moment, the profile of the consummate team player. His or her personality attributes are as follows:

1.　There is a very high need for nurturance. This has been found to be quite critical to team success. The team member wants to have the approval of his teammates and of the crowd as well. That approval is highly motivating to the success of the individual as he operates within the framework of the team. One more important finding in studies of successful teams was the homogeneity required in the need for nurturance. If a team is composed of members who have similar needs for nurturance it will succeed more often than a team in which there are wide discrepancies in the need for nurturance among the players. One can imagine that the more homogeneous the needs of a team, the easier it is for the coach and teammates to know how to motivate each other. If a team had a few loners and a few players with high needs for nurturance, there might be resentment by the latter of the former who neither give nor need to receive praise.

2.　Team players are typically highly empathic, that is, if their team is to be a winning one. It appears that to win at a team effort, you must be tuned in to the emotional signals of others and sensitive to the responses given by teammates. Emotional coordination yields a team that not only operates as one but feels as one too.

3. Winning team members have what behavioral scientists call a high need for affiliation. They thrive best in circumstances where they interact with others and are accepted as part of the group.

One last difference between the team and individual winner is that the latter tends to be a more introverted and dominant personality while the former tends to be more extroverted and more self-effacing. To win at team endeavors, it appears one has to be an able communicator and one who does so in a humble way. The solo player, with some notable exceptions such as Muhammed Ali, is introverted, inflexible and dominant. We are all witness to that embarrassing sports television ritual: the interview of the victor after the event in which we are definitely convinced that solo sports champions are not natural communicators. That's because they are both introverted and dominant and so they have little to say, don't know how to say it and aren't convinced that it needs saying.

The team player is more likely to put him or herself in the background, giving others credit, subordinating individual accomplishment to team effort and articulating feelings effectively. Howard Cosell take note! Your best postgame interviews will be with football players, not boxers. In industry, the problem becomes even more crucial.

People who are promoted to positions of leadership in a business organization may come from different parts of the organization. Some travel the fast track through sales and marketing. Others find their way to the top via the legal department or accounting.

Imagine, for a moment, the differences in personality between the team-based marketing executive who is made president of the company and a lone-wolf attorney who has reached the same position. The latter may have distinguished himself in a largely solitary environment of legal briefs, contractual analysis and the like. Here we would have a solo winner, now, as president, being asked to take over a team operation. There might be serious problems and there sometimes are when this type of person is selected to lead an organization.

In my experience consulting to corporations, the companies with the most difficulty in morale and client relations are those in which numerous attorneys and accountants have made it to the top. The leopard doesn't change his spots when he gets the corner office and has reached top rung in the organization. So many chief executives in this predicament either fail or desperately hire consultants to help them understand the team they now head and which they must now address and lead. They buy consulting services to teach them how to make speeches; how to understand the emotional climate of the organization; and how to build a team out of disparate talents in the organization. The chief executive who comes from a team background such as marketing may not have nearly the same problem. He or she is usually a far more capable and intuitive leader of people. But, alas, life has a down side for the team player, too. The solo player, you remember, was a more dominant person and needed less nurturance from others. Hence, this type of leader is more comfortable making hard and unpopular decisions that might benefit the organization in the long run. The team player may try to lead by consensus, even when the times call for a benevolent dictatorship.

Take the following test to assess your own need for people and interpersonal style:

                                                                    T   F

1. I feel comfortable receiving presents.
2. I feel bad when I accidentaly interrupt someone who is speaking.
3. I try hard to tune in to what people expect of me and try hard to deliver.
4. I would say that my friends really know what irritates me.
5. I believe in giving the underdog a break.
6. I am a "joiner" and belong to one or more voluntary organizations.
7. I enjoy socializing with friends and family and do so at least part of every weekend.

Analysis of Results

Each "True" answer puts you in the category of a team player and each "False" answer says you are more like a solo competitor. Don't try to change if you choose not to. You can be a success either way. What's critical, however, is that you are aware of what your style is and don't become a fish out of water. If you are a team player, head in that direction in your business and personal life. If you do best as a solo, there is much you can accomplish that way. Maybe you'll make a less popular leader than someone else, but you'll be more capable of making the hard yet necessary decisions. Maybe you shouldn't strive for leadership at all and, instead, remain content to reap success as a solo act. Either way, if you know what you do best, you'll be much more likely to succeed.

7
THE FLESH IS WILLING
Physical Health

If there is a Success Factor, is it a phenomenon of the mind alone or does it affect the body as well? Are successful people better endowed to begin with from a physical as well as intellectual standpoint?

As a child psychiatrist, I have watched this issue debated over the twenty years I have practiced. The traditional school of thought adheres to the stereotype of the bright student. He or she is a "bookworm," myopic, freckle-faced, hunched over with bones that would break if he or she sneezed too hard.

True enough, many studious people are not physically fit, but this might be due to neglect instead of poor endowment. After all, if you spend hours each day over your books or computer, the muscles in your belly won't develop a firmness that makes them ripple when you stand on the beach. Is a hard-edged intellect necessarily associated with a flabby body?

There is another school of thought that rejects the stereotype of the feeble-bodied intellectual. Its conclusions come from the observation of thousands of normal children whose physical and emotional development have been followed over many years in research studies of various types. These studies have produced data that is the antithesis of the stereotype described above. In these research projects it was found that there is usually a strong correlation between superior intellectual and physical endowment. Some people have all the luck! Makes you want to believe in reincarnation, doesn't it? Maybe I'll be one of those lucky ones next time around.

In any case, the superior mind is usually connected to a superior body but, as we discussed earlier, that body could be neglected and allowed to deteriorate. To have a higher probability of success, it's best to take care of both body and mind. The well-tuned body feeds energy to a superior mind which then can devise winning intellectual strategies. Ask any executive who populates a health spa catering to industry what the result of an hour's exercise is on the work to be performed the rest of the day. The answer is bound to be that physical exertion is a bracing stimulant to achievement. Numerous companies, recognizing this, have built gymnasiums on site or subsidize their executives if they subscribe to local health spas. Let's see if the evidence for a connection between fitness and success goes beyond a turn on the exercise bicycle.

A study was done on patients suffering from rheumatoid arthritis. This highly disabling illness is a progressive one that occurs in young people as well as the elderly and leads to progressive restriction of joint movement, swelling and deformities of the fingers and other joints and, ultimately, may be fatal. Clearly these sufferers must watch their step when it comes to physical movement lest they overdo it and further damage their joints. True? Not at all!

The results of an important study on patients who overcame their handicap versus those whose disease became progressively more disabling showed that those people who had higher self-esteem, higher social activity and higher levels of attempted physical activity were those who were successful in overcoming their handicap. It seems that the mind is capable of infusing the body with a healing process just as a well-tuned body is capable of sparking the mind into action. Scientists who study the relationship of the mind to disease make no distinction anymore between the mind and body, seeing both as aspects of the same entity—the self. Makes you believe what the Indian gurus have preached for centuries, doesn't it? They have long held that a troubled mind will interfere with the healing process and have developed meditation as a remedy. They also have held that the body is the temple of the mind and it must be treated with the dignity it deserves. Perhaps, the next time you see someone with a dot in the middle of his forehead and a turban on his head, you will recall the fact that his culture has much to teach us when it comes to understanding the relationship of mind, body and living a successful life.

A very important study was performed on dog-sled racers. Both physical and psychological tests were performed and the results were cross-tabulated to compare winners and also-rans. Winners in the dog-sled races had two significant differences from other competitors. They scored higher on an honesty scale and they showed fewer ill effects to the body from the wear and tear of the race; a manifestation of better physical conditioning.

Well, it's easy to understand how physical conditioning plays a role in winning a dogsled race. But, honesty? Again, the results of the research on successes of all types throws us a curve. Just when we were getting to wish that successful people had some fatal flaw, a series of studies from India to Alaska prove that the successful person is more perfect, even morally, than the rest of us. What is the significance of honesty in winning an athletic contest? Let's study winning further to find out.

You are, no doubt, familiar with Drs. Friedman and Rosenman and their famous study of the Type A personality. As you know, they found the Type A, a person who reacts with compulsive aggression to any and all issues, to be much more highly vulnerable to heart attacks. The Type B, by contrast, they found to be more laid back and less prone to heart disease. However, since their landmark study, it has been found that there are at least two subgroups of Type A. The first is the highly vulnerable one with the knee-jerk aggressive response. The second is less vulnerable to heart disease and is someone who is competently aggressive. Such are the subjects of the study to be discussed next.

This study of students who were classed as either Type A or Type B with regard to the characteristics that have been known to predict cardiac risk factors showed the following:

1. The "reformed" Type A's took on greater challenges.
2. They coped better.
3. They reported no greater stress than people who took on lesser challenges.
4. Their blood chemistries showed changes which correlate with people who feel stress but have it under control.

Let's put this study together with the last one (the dogsled findings) and see if we can illuminate the winner's profile a little bit better.

The winning competitor (a "reformed" Type A, usually) is faced with a series of challenges. He or she decides to shoot for the top and takes on the most impressive challenge. The resources for coping are as follows:

■ On the psychological side we have honesty and a sense of control over the situation. The honesty trait is what makes the winner face up to his or her limitations and fears. The Type A aggression is what makes the winner overcome these and take charge of the situation.
■ On the physical side we have great physical conditioning. This is what provides the energy and stamina to propel the winner to the summit of achievement.

Together, mind, body and personality combine to help the competitor cope more efficiently and, consequently, to feel less stress. As you can see, the winner is someone who is active, faces stress and challenges and doesn't indulge in self-delusion or deceit. We are describing the ultimate straight shooter. We are also describing a consistent winner.

If you want to be a winner, your Success Factor must include a well-conditioned body, a calm disposition (helped by meditation or biofeedback), and honest recognition of the nature of the challenge facing you and an adventurous spirit that prefers being involved in "main events" rather than in sideshows.

8

THE EINSTEIN COMPLEX
Intelligence and Creativity

Just as important as what I have found in my extensive review of the world literature on success is what I did not find. Nowhere, for example, was I able to find a correlation between genius and success.

There is a commonly held belief that people who make it big are in a category superior to the rest of us from an intellectual point of view. Granted, it helps to be smart. But the intelligence possessed by people who have been able to follow the ideas in this book thus far is enough to make you a huge success. You don't have to be an Einstein to be a success. I meet as many MENSA members who drive taxis in New York City as I do when I attend upscale parties on the posh Upper East Side of Manhattan. Being a genius is no guarantee of success in life. Yet, there are certain qualities of intelligence that are crucial to achievement.

One factor is verbal comprehension. Interestingly, the emphasis is on "comprehension" and not "expression." Apparently, listening to and comprehending others is crucial to success. This shouldn't come as a surprise to most of us. You've seen advertisements stressing how some companies conduct staff education programs to enhance listening skills.

Sperry Rand Corporation has featured such ads for years. Other companies have similarly focused on teaching executives to listen to employee and consumer issues through a variety of means. One such device is the attitude survey. I'd like to share with you an experience I had some time ago with a company that performed an attitude survey on its employees and found, to its dismay, that it needed a psychiatrist badly.

Several years ago I was asked to consult to a large corporation having difficulties on two fronts. First, its employees had become less and less productive each year for the last decade for no apparent reason. Second, the company was experiencing great difficulties in client relations; the customers increasingly opposed its prices and resisted, on environmental grounds, the opening of a partly completed multibillion-dollar plant. I decided to begin my study of the situation with an analysis of the communication patterns in the company.

First, I did a survey of the employees' level of trust in various sources of company information. I found that employees typically did not trust any information they read in the company newspaper. They trusted a bit more in the information conveyed via formal channels through the company hierarchy in the form of memos and notices. They trusted most in the "grapevine." Hence, from the outset it was clear that the more "official" the communication, the less it was trusted as reflecting true company operating policy. In effect, employees felt that what management said formally was a lie, and the only true source of information about management's intentions was what could be gleaned through gossip. "How could this be?" top managers asked me. "This isn't the way it was twenty years ago when I started out in this company."

"Tell me the way it was when you first came to work here," I asked one of the senior vice presidents.

With a nostalgic look of contentment in his eyes, he recounted, "It used to be like a big happy family back then. We knew the company was going to be our home forever. We gave it all we had and knew we would be taken care of in times of trouble." With that, he proceeded to describe numerous cases in which employees, in times of need, had turned to the company for support and pointed out that it was never denied.

"Sounds like one big happy family," I agreed. "Do you think I could speak with some of the employees out in the field and get their points of view?"

"Sure," he readily assented and arranged for me to travel to a division of the company located several hundred miles from headquarters to interview a broad cross section of the staff confidentially.

My meetings with the staff were an eye-opener. As an emissary of management, at first I felt I might need a bullet-proof vest, such was the hostility and mistrust expressed towards "head office." I dissociated myself with management, indicating that I was an agent for solving the problem, not an ally of any faction. Probably because I look and act like I would make such an inept manager, I was believed and my credentials as a behavioral scientist were accepted.

After a few hesitant beginnings by several disgruntled employees, a torrent of complaints, bitterness and frustration was unleashed. One burly man with a red, weather-beaten face began to gesture with a hand the size of a frying pan and probably just as hard. "You asked us what grieves us? First of all, even if I'm ready to believe you give a damn, I don't believe the company gives two hoots about what bothers us. They want production from us and that's it. 'Do your job and shut the fuck up' is their attitude."

Noting that many others in the group were nodding their assent as he spoke, I asked, "Can you give me some examples of how that attitude of management gets expressed on the job? Can you tell me what they do that makes you feel that they want you to speak only when spoken to?"

The man with frying-pan hands was silent as he looked around for help from others in the group. An Oriental man who had been silent to that point spoke up. "The company just put in a centralized computer system. What this has done is to take all decision-making out of our hands and locate it in headquarters. Well maybe those lawyers who run things up there need to control everything, but they don't know the havoc it creates down here."

As he spoke, I could see others bursting with examples to corroborate his point. A slim, elderly man with a distinguished Southern drawl spoke next. "I've been with the company twenty-seven years. I've been a loyal company man all these years. But now, I think things are daft here. I'll give you an example. The company stresses economy. That means, no new equipment. Make do with what you have. O.K., but then, when we try to do that, we are breaking company rules."

"How so?" I asked.

"Well, last month my crew needed a back hoe for a certain job. We didn't have one and I knew we couldn't get one if it was requisitioned because of the austerity drive by head office. So I took a couple of cars we didn't need and asked Jerry if he would trade me a back hoe he had no use for against the cars which he needed."

Looking across the room, I saw Jerry nod his head in agreement and then his brow furrowed in consternation. "Looks like a good idea," I said, "what went wrong?"

The old veteran continued. "Headquarters did a routine inventory check and nailed us for the trade. We had broken a company rule about assignment of equipment. Apparently, if I didn't need two cars, I was to return them to H.Q. If Jerry didn't need a back hoe, he was to do likewise. Then, both of us were supposed to put a requisition into the God-damned computer and play mix-and-match to see if the machine would make the swap. Well, I'll tell you, doc, had we done that, we'd never have gotten the equipment we needed and the job wouldn't have gotten done. You can't win for losing around here."

A further analysis of field employee experience revealed numerous similar experiences. The newly implemented centralization scheme that was supposed to streamline operations and trim cost was not trusted by employees. That fact was not recognized by top management. I went back to headquarters and asked how much time had been spent by head office staff explaining the new system in the field. "In fact," I asked, "how much time do executives spend in the field, getting to know the grievances of employees, socializing with and getting to know their spouses and sharing head office concerns and strategies?"

A red-faced and embarrassed executive vice president answered, "Not much at all. We have become so preoccupied with financial and regulatory issues, we have forgotten to perpetuate what was once great about this company: the family feeling we used to share." He vowed to implement immediately a new set of priorities, including weekly trips to the district for informal talks with employees to air grievances; listening to and implementing their cost-saving suggestions; and showing employees, through empathic listening, that they still had an important role to play in the "family."

The results were dramatic and immediate. Productivity in the district, near the bottom in the corporation until then, soared to the top. Consumer relations improved dramatically, as would be expected. When employees are disgruntled with their own management, they pass on this irritation to consumers. When employees feel proud to be considered a part of the "family," their pride is conveyed to consumers in the spirit and manner in which they conduct their job.

This company learned the importance of empathic listening in order to be successful. Computers can't listen to people. They only record data. Company newsletters and memos don't communicate with people. They only disseminate words. Communication is only possible when a person who cares about another person takes the time to listen and comprehend. Only then does a computer's data become meaningful and can a company's newsletter or memo be trusted.

It didn't surprise me, then, when I discovered in my search of the literature that the item "verbal comprehension" was highly associated with success. I would only add that, in order for words to have meaning or be truly comprehended, the listener must be empathic and hear the feelings behind the words. One last example to make this point.

We all participate in the morning ritual of reading the newspaper. If asked, I'm sure you'd claim that you understand each and every word you read. On one level that's true. But that's not the end of verbal comprehension.

I'm sure you've read, in the past, about a tragic fire that claimed several lives. You read the description of what happened and then turned the page to see what was playing at the movies and which team won last night's hockey game. Words convey ideas but not necessarily understanding. Imagine, now, that you are actually at the fire. You watch a mother scream at firemen, "My children are up there," pointing to the third floor of the tenement building and struggling against the restraint of firemen who know it is futile for her or themselves to try to rescue the children at this point. You see the terror in the mother's eyes; the sadness, helplessness and compassion of the firemen; and the bewilderment of the passers-by. Finally, you see several soot-stained faces in firemen's uniforms emerge from the tenement with rubber bags containing the dead bodies of children. You see the mother collapse with grief and a veteran fireman break down and weep. Now you "comprehend" what has gone on when the newspaper says that several people died in a fire. You are not inclined to look to the movie page or check out the hockey score.

People who are successful in life have an extraordinary capacity for empathic listening. They have verbal comprehension skills to the fullest meaning of those words. Because they understand more deeply, events have a more profound impact upon them and they, in turn, are more equipped to understand and respond to events.

There are some less lofty applications of the capacity to comprehend empathically. A study of high school students showed that the more successful ones used their capacity to comprehend empathically to win popularity by verbal seduction. The more deeply you understand other people's feelings, the more easily you can manipulate them, if you choose to.

A separate study of children in a Head Start program was revealing as well. It tracked verbal comprehension and assessed future success. The findings were predictable in light of what we now know. The better the skill at verbal comprehension at the preschool level, the greater the future success. Apparently, this correlation holds true for success prediction wherever we look.

What about other intellectual abilities? Is verbal comprehension the only one of significance when it comes to predicting success? Apparently not.

A special kind of memory skill has been found to correlate with success. There are several ways to test memory. You can show people an item or a series of items and see, later on, if they can recognize what they were shown. In the same way, you can explain a concept to someone and see if they recognize the concept later on. When this is done, both successful people and unsuccessful people score the same on recognition of concepts at a later date. But when asked to recall, explain and utilize rather than merely recognize a concept discussed earlier, only successful people score highly. Is this merely a recall phenomenon, some quirk of memory that some are endowed with genetically? I would suggest not. Recall the earlier discussion on empathic verbal comprehension. If you are open to more than the words and ideas, letting the emotional significance of the information have an impact on you, you will fully recall concepts, not just recognizing them but understanding and applying them as well. A personal example will illustrate this point.

When I was studying to get into medical school, I knew that high grades were what would get me in the door. I studied all subjects from that standpoint alone. I simply wanted to retain as much information as possible and be able to regurgitate it on demand at exam time. It worked. I was accepted to a highly competitive medical school. However, once in, I realized that people's lives would depend upon how well I was able to apply the information I was studying. A drastic change in strategy came into my study habits. I would visualize a real, sick person behind every idea I was learning. I soon adopted the tactic of going to the hospital to seek out, on the wards, someone who had the condition I was studying in my textbook. I would sit awhile, talking to the person, discovering that he had just become a grandfather, that he had dreams about retiring to San Diego and that he was a great tennis player in his youth. Only then did the fact of his emphysema have meaning to me. How would it affect his tennis game, or his dreams of retiring to San Diego or the life he planned to share with his grandchildren? It became a lot easier to remember the signs and symptoms of emphysema after that experience. The words in the textbook recalled his face and the hope it held for the future. From then on, it became impossible to forget the complex treatments prescribed in the textbook.

Another intellectual capacity is strongly associated with success. That is low distractibility. Clearly, winners have the ability to stick to the task and are not easily separated from it by trivial or even important distractions. This may be an intellectual capacity of its own or it might be associated with empathic verbal comprehension as well. After seeing the children trapped in a fire, the fireman would find himself unlikely to be distracted by anything the next time the fire alarm rang at the stationhouse. After discussing my patient's dreams for his future in San Diego, his love for his grandchildren and his abilities as a tennis player, and then watching as he struggled to breathe due to his emphysema, I would not easily be distracted when I heard someone complain of the symptoms of emphysema.

The last attribute of a successful mind is imagination and creativity. Here, too, there is a connection with empathic listening. I don't know which comes first: the ability to listen with feeling or a piercingly sensitive, creative and imaginative intellect that makes empathy possible. But they are attributes that always seem to go together in successful people. Only an empathic person can tune in to the essence of a situation or concept. By doing so, one becomes capable of expressing it esthetically, conceptually or verbally—three aspects of creativity. Interestingly, when you study successful people from all walks of life, you find superior esthetic/creative capacities. This holds true if you study students, business people or athletes. Apparently, to be successful, you must not only have special intellectual, physical, emotional and personality skills, but you must use them more creatively than others.

Einstein made the rest of us feel a little more stupid. To this day, when I think of the space/time continuum, curved space or the fact that as velocity increases, time slows down, I feel like sucking my thumb. I have coined a new term, describing a new neurosis which I think will rival the Oedipus Complex or the Electra Complex in importance. It is the "Einstein Complex." It afflicts those of us who break out into a sweat and become short of breath when we see a computer for the first time, see a friend smile as he deftly describes an algorithm or asks you if you're familiar with the "C" programming language. Anyone whose hands tremble when exposed to such stresses has the Einstein Complex and may use this as an excuse for going to sleep for a week, breaking out into hives or even committing murder. But the Einstein Complex will never be an excuse for not succeeding. You only need to let the full impact of what you hear be known to both your heart and your mind. Then it can have maximum impact on you, allowing you to respond creatively, empathically, intelligently and successfully.

9
SUCCESS, IS IT YOUR BIRTHRIGHT?

When you speak with very successful people, you hear one recollection over and over again. They all say, "I knew from the time I was very young that I was special in some way and that I would do big things when I got older. I didn't know quite what I would be, but I knew I wouldn't lead an ordinary life." So it seems that some people have success in their bloodstream from a very early age. Call it intuition, or a gift, or, if you believe in reincarnation, knowledge from another life. But there are some of us who know we are destined for higher things long before we attain maturity.

Researchers haven't systematically studied the minds of such children to understand what makes them think this way. But clinical observation is helpful. Experience with gifted patients has shown that there are some aspects of development so far ahead of any others that they stick out like a sore thumb, making it unmistakably obvious to the child and to those around that this is no ordinary little person.

Take the case of Jules, an accomplished cellist. He recalled in one of our therapy sessions how, when he was a young boy of three, he would listen to symphonies his father would play on their stereo and was able to remember every note, every

harmony and vividly recreate the entire score in his mind
after just one exposure to the music. Surely this is the
auditory equivalent of a photographic memory.

Jules would also be able to sit at the piano, an instrument
whose keyboard he could hardly reach, and play tunes with
full bass accompaniment without benefit of even one lesson.
His friends, by comparison, would hardly be able to play
Chopsticks after trying numerous times.

In other respects, he was also superior, including in
academics and at sports. But no trait stood out as prominently
as did his musical talent. While he knew he was generally superior to the kids around him because he could so easily
outperform them on most levels, he knew his musical
aptitude was nothing short of magical. He remembered being
troubled by this as well as getting pleasure from it.

"I remember," he remarked, "how I would want to write
down musical creations that were on my mind but I couldn't
even spell my name. My mind's ear would hear the most
sophisticated melodies with full orchestral arrangements but
I couldn't recreate them or save them for others to appreciate.
I felt like my mind was a magical musical sieve, first receiving,
then losing precious musical experiences. When I took cello
lessons, I couldn't buckle down and learn to read music for a
long time because I couldn't read as quickly as I could play by
ear. I grew impatient with trying to read notes when I already
could play any tune by ear."

"What about other kids," I asked, "did you get along well
with them?"

"Yes and no," he recalled painfully. "If I faked like I was one
of them, I was O.K. But often I would get frustrated because I
knew so much more than I could do, musically and socially. I
would get irritable and not want to be around my peers."

Anna Freud, some years ago, described what Jules experienced. She discovered that children develop at an uneven
rate. For some, motor development shoots out ahead of intellectual development. Others have intellects that strike out
boldly while their physical development lags behind. For
some, sexual development outpaces social skills. In all cases,
severe strains may arise. The girl with budding sexuality who

can't handle a relationship gets pregnant to strengthen her hold on a boyfriend she fears she is not good enough to keep otherwise. The boy whose mind can outreach his physical prowess learns to be grandiose with friends to boost his fragile ego. The girl whose physical abilities outpace her mental capacity takes foolish risks that may lead to a serious injury.

Eventually, development smoothes out these differences and there is harmony between the mind, the body, the sexual urges and relationships. But, until that happens, the child feels frustrated and may renounce a gift that can't be handled. This repudiation may last a lifetime. Hence, many of us have exceptional traits that lie buried under layers of maturation, much like an ancient civilization with treasure of untold magnitude lies undiscovered for centuries, overgrown by vegetation and overbuilt by a contemporary civilization that obscures the first.

To recover your birthright of talent, you often have to dig deep into childhood to unearth what was exceptional and revive it. Some people have an easier time of it.

Researchers have shown that some people have a greater probability of fulfilling their potential without the risk of it being buried under years of strain and neglect. These are:

1. People whose parents are educated or who value education
2. People whose mothers were in a high socioeconomic class
3. People who are born in urban areas or who live there in later life
4. First born (94% of the astronauts are first born)
5. Women whose mothers broke from traditional sex roles and pursued "males-only" careers
6. Women who, as children, were "daddy's girl"

Some of the reasons for these children having greater success in later life are obvious. High socioeconomic status of a mother might imply (although I don't know this for a fact) that educational values are held very high in that parent. It is thought that the mother is the parent with more influence over the child in the early, formative years. Hence, her interest in education would be transmitted to her children.

Birth or later residence in an urban area might have a salutory effect on realizing potential because of the intense cultural stimulation of city life.

First born are ground breakers from the start. In my pediatric clinical days we always used to observe how it was so much easier for second children than for first born. On-the-job training for a parent of a first child may make it tough on the child but it also makes for a tough child, hardy and pioneering in both early and later years.

Women whose mothers pursued non-traditionally female occupations have a role model that says, "Break the rules. Be what you want to be." These children are more likely to assert their full potential, regardless of the strain it causes within themselves or with their peers.

Women who are reared under daddy's wing might do the same, led on by the father's image as a "doer."

High achievement is the birthright of most of us. However, for reasons beyond our control, our greatest talents may have been suppressed by peer pressure, shamed into hiding by parents who didn't respect and even ridiculed a gift, lulled to sleep by a too laid-back environment, or bound and gagged by traditions and rules that have kept women (and men) "in their place," kept minorities out of the "private club" or emphasized less valuable abilities that are "more acceptable in our circles."

To retrieve and reclaim your birthright of success, you should recall your first remembered skill. That is probably your most innately valuable asset. You should also remember what you most enjoyed when you were an adolescent. Your most durable ability is one that successfully made it through the development storms into young adulthood. I'll bet that you aren't using either your earliest skill or your adolescent abilities in your current work. It's time to become an anthropologist and go on a dig. Only, in this case, you are the site of the expedition and the ancient treasure you seek is the long forgotten or neglected ability that might now become your royal road to success.

WORKSHOP I
Defining Success

It's hard to throw darts and get a bull's-eye if you don't know where the target is. You might hit the mark, but it would be pure chance if you did. When you aim for success, you need to know how to define your target in order to direct your aim.

Age/Stage

It's absurd to expect a three-month-old infant to walk. Yet at thirteen months, it's normal to have that expectation. It would be even more ridiculous to expect the three-month-old to run or climb a tree before he or she learned to walk. For every goal in life, there is an age at which you become ready to succeed, an age where it is premature to expect to succeed, and an age at which succeeding at the goal is irrelevant. You wouldn't feel it to be too significant if your teenager said, "Look Ma, I can walk!"

Most goals are part of a sequence of achievements with necessary precursor stages and subsequent stages that are made possible by the completion of the given stage. So, walking is preceded by crawling which strengthens the muscles of the limbs. Then balance, a new skill, is attained and the child learns to walk. When the child learns to chase his center of gravity and deal with the kinetic energy of the body in rapid movement, then he can learn how to run.

For every success goal, there are these requirements:

1. Precursor stage(s)
2. Precursor ability(ies)
3. New ability(ies) to be developed
4. New challenges to conquer

Simply applied, this should mean that for learning to run, we would require:

1. Walking
2. Knowing how to balance the body in an erect position
3. Learning how to chase one's center of gravity at high speed and how to deal with kinetic energy of the body as it changes direction.
4. Running at high speed

Now, for each goal you wish to attain, fill in the following:

1. The stage I must complete prior to attaining the new goal
2. The fundamental skills that I must have already acquired at this stage before going on to the new goal
3. The new skills I must acquire in order to reach the new goal
4. The new challenge I seek to master

The Art of the Possible

Ask any successful person about his or her career and you will find it has had many false starts and failures. Getting up off your back and starting over can be easy or discouraging, depending on your point of view. If you set goals and then try to swallow them whole, you'll gag and choke on the task of trying to succeed. Success can only be digested in small bites just as failure can best be handled in small doses. If you set goals with small easy steps leading toward your objectives, it will be easier to cope with each step and each setback will be minimal and tolerable.

Take any goal you wish to attain at the present moment. Break it up into small steps. For each step, anticipate at least two possible glitches and specify how you would overcome these obstacles.

GOAL		PROBLEM	SOLUTION
STEP 1	1)		
	2)		
STEP 2	1)		
	2)		
STEP 3	1)		
	2)		
STEP 4	1)		
	2)		
STEP 5	1)		
	2)		

If solving the problem can't be done in five steps, take ten or twenty or as many as you need. Breaking the problem down makes it more accessible, less forbidding and makes temporary failure less frightening. An example is in order.

When I was first assigned as ward chief in a department of psychiatry, I noticed that the nurses spent the smallest amount of time with the sickest patients and devoted the greatest amount of effort to the healthiest ones. I analyzed the situation through observation and discussion with the nursing staff and discovered that the reason the sickest patients were avoided was due to the sense of hopelessness the nurses had about their recovery.

"It takes so much out of me to spend time with Carl," said one very compassionate nurse.

"Why?" I inquired.

"Because no matter what you do, he just stares off into space like you don't even exist," she replied. "I try and try to get him to respond but the most I can get him to do is look back at me when I'm there. Apart from eye contact, he can't do any communicating."

Excited, I said, "You mean you could get Carl to make eye contact with you? That's great. Did you tell him you think it's a real step forward to see him look at you and share his feelings with you that way?"

"Well...well no, not really," she replied.

"I'd acknowledge each step forward he made, however small, and reward him with your attention and your enthusiasm," I advised. "Let's break down the steps between where he is now, mute and uncommunicative, and where you want him to be. See if you can acknowledge each small step he makes toward the goal of speaking freely with you and let him set the timetable for attaining each new step along the way."

The nurse proceeded to follow this plan and Carl began to communicate within one week. By making his progress accessible to her, even though each step was infinitessimally small, she developed enthusiasm for him, stopped neglecting him and in this way both patient and nurse reached their objectives.

While my example, as with most of my experience, is derived from a clinical background, the principles hold true in all other settings, be it child-rearing, helping out a subordinate or encouraging your spouse to attain new heights. If you break down the objective into manageable steps, the process becomes one of multiple small successes. If you look for giant leaps forward, you end up with major dis-appointments. Give me a small victory better than a big failure any time.

Internal versus External Goals

In establishing your goals, you must make them please two masters:

1. Your internal needs
2. The people in your life who hold the key to the next step forward

If you please one and not the other, stagnation eventually results. Failure to please yourself leads to burnout. Failure to recognize that there are people in your life with whom you must come to terms if you are to get ahead leads to a ghetto philosophy for one's career. If you ignore or feel hostile towards your boss, co-workers or clients and take the attitude, "I'm the expert; public opinion be damned," then your ship will sink rather than come in. To navigate to a successful career, you need to know and follow the rules, even though you are the captain of your own life.

List your major goals at present and in the near future. See if you can name an internal need each satisfies and also if each goal will win you recognition from those in your life who can help you advance.

GOAL	INTERNAL NEED	EXTERNAL REWARD
1)		
2)		
3)		
4)		
5)		

The Winning Mindset

Along with setting a winning objective for yourself, you must learn to visualize yourself as a person capable of attaining that goal. In other words, you must learn to see yourself as a "sure thing." You will recall, in the research studies quoted elsewhere in this book, it was discovered that people who had a stubborn attitude about winning and couldn't visualize themselves as losing, even in the face of certain failure, seemed to win consistently more than "more reasonable" folks who could "see the writing on the wall" and would give up when failure loomed. Having an uncompromising attitude about winning seems to be a necessary emergency resource when all else fails. If time, money, reason and even the facts run out on you, what will pull you through to success is a stubborn, maybe even crazy, adherence to your self-image as a "sure winner."

I recall a recent tennis match in which the champion was down two sets to none and was at the wall with match point against him. Somehow, he staved off certain defeat, went on to win the game, the set and, eventually, the match. When his opponent was interviewed on television and asked how he analyzed the match, especially his opponent's comeback, he said, "That's the difference between a champion and the rest of us. The champion will simply not accept failure."

An analysis of success should include the following:

1. A positive self-image as a "sure winner"
2. The appropriate age and stage: the right time and sequence for each goal
3. The art of the possible: how you will succeed in stages
4. The internal and external rewards you hope to achieve

When you have been able to work through this analysis of success for yourself with the detail and clarity recommended in this workshop, you will be in a position to set out on an aggressive quest to meet and conquer all your objectives.

━━━━━━━━━━ WORKSHOP II
Getting Set for the Journey

Taking a journey to an unknown place is always exciting, also scary. That's why we do it so seldom in a lifetime. Instead, we become creatures of habit and gravitate back to the same vacation spot year after year. "How about a safari to Africa?" you ask yourself and then answer, "Well, maybe next year. This year, I think I'll go back to the lake."

The only time of life in which adventure into the unknown is intensely desired is adolescence. During this growth phase, the child, emerging into adulthood, seeks to explore all the territory previously denied to him in childhood. There is an insatiable need to master the unknown. That's what makes adolescence so exciting for the child going through that phase. It's also what gives parents grey hair as we watch our teenagers constantly going off into unknown places with nothing but curiosity, intelligence and desire to rely on.

The quest for success in adulthood strongly resembles the adolescent's plunge into the unknown. An entrepreneur, seeking his or her fortune, has only curiosity, intelligence and desire as resources. Admittedly, there may be a reserve of money and experience in the background, but the unique resources of the entrepreneur that make for success where others fail are the curiosity to explore the unknown, the intelligence to think things through as problems arise, and drive, ambition or desire for success.

The journey into the unknown world of superachievement is apt to frighten us adults. After all, we know how foolish adolescents are to try to take on the world single-handedly. We realize how important it is to have some guarantees in advance of how things might turn out before running off on a trip to nowhere with friends or changing career choices precipitously. Adolescents are used to taking risks and expecting things to turn out all right. We caution our adolescents to turn to us for help as soon as they run into trouble; we advise them to go slow; we implore them not to make abrupt decisions. They keep us in the dark, make snap decisions, and change career preferences as often as a bumblebee prospecting for pollen in the summer hops from flower to flower. And they master the unknown that way.

If you want to succeed on your journey to high achievement, you have to go back and think more like you did in your adolescence. It's time to rely, once again, on guts, desire and a mind that believes it knows it all or, at least, a mind that can get to know whatever is important as the need arises. You have to shake things up a bit in your life, break some rules, grow cocky and "go for it" like an adolescent. It's natural for an adolescent to be hell-bent on becoming the best track star, movie star, motorcycle racer, fashion model or any other goal the adolescent mind can conjure. For the adolescent, most of these ambitions are premature and end up as unfulfilled dreams. For you, there is one difference: you really are in a position to rise to the top of your field, if you choose. Combining the adolescent's "go for broke" attitude with adult capabilities is the surest way to succeed. In order to renew that adolescent zeal, you have to make a few changes in your usual way of thinking and acting.

1.   *You've got to release old inhibitions.* It's important to get rid of guilts, traditions and useless rules that might stop the momentum before it gets started.

2.   *You need to strengthen your internal locus of control.* You are going off on your own with only your instincts to guide you. It's important to learn to rely on inner resources and take

responsibility for the path you choose and the outcome you achieve.

3. *You need a stubborn dream.* It's important to have a tenacious idea that just won't let go of your imagination. This will be your continuing inspiration to go forward no matter what the resistance.

Getting rid of old guilts is easy.

Ask yourself who instilled this guilt in you. Do you still want that person running a little tyranny in your mind? If not, cancel the lease, evict the unwanted tenant in your mind, replace the old rules with new ones of your own creation. We often give our parents or the other people who influenced us in childhood a lifelong lease to reside inside our consciences. Sometimes it works out. The tenant behaves and lives by the rules of our household. Other times, the internalized parent, residing permanently in the conscience, causes havoc with our lives. There comes a time when you have a right not to renew the lease.

When you have decided to take over your own conscience once again, you can set rules for your life that work rather than cause guilt for you.

To strengthen your internal locus of control, you must learn to reinterpret everything in your life from the standpoint of your own responsibility. Try the following:

1. List the most important achievements and failures of your life.

   a)

   b)

   c)

   d)

   e)

   f)

2. For each item listed above, write a sentence or two describing your own contribution to the achievement or failure.

   a)

   b)

   c)

   d)

   e)

   f)

3. For each contribution you made to a success or failure in your life, define the quality in you that caused you to act the way you did.

   a)

   b)

   c)

   d)

   e)

   f)

Now, as an example, if you succeeded in getting a promotion, you might have brought this about by making your accomplishments visible. The personal trait of expressiveness and maybe even exhibitionism might have helped you achieve this success.

If you had a failure such as losing an important client, the contribution you could have made to that failure might have been taking his business for granted. Your personality trait that could have caused you to take the client's business for granted might have been lack of empathy.

If you do this exercise, you will develop a list of personality traits that help and hinder your career. You will soon learn the traits that need strengthening and attributes which need to be valued in your personality. These resources are vital to you in attaining success. They must not go unrecognized while you assume your successes or failures are due to good or bad luck.

Acquiring a stubborn dream, I'm afraid to say, is an impossible task. You either have one or you don't. You either believe in miracles or you believe in transistors and adding machines. It's that simple. Most of us can believe in dreams. Yet, too many of us have forgotten our most important ones. They are trashed as soon as we receive our first payment book on the new car and realize that there is an inescapable reality connected to dreams—responsibility. As soon as we realize that Santa Claus or good ol' dad won't pick up the tab any more, we angrily abandon the dream. How often have you felt, "Well, if I have to ask you for something, it loses its appeal. I don't want it any more." Apparently, even the task of having to ask for a dream to come true is too onerous a burden for some people to carry. So, when they pick up adult responsibility, they throw their dreams in the ash can.

Dreams and work must go hand in hand. Adult dreams come true only with hard work. Adult dreams are stubborn dreams. They grip the mind like a bulldog with teeth clenched on the mailman's trouser cuff. They howl in the night, waking you up out of a sleep, leaving you agitated, but in a creative state, ready to work all night, if need be, to figure out a new way to achieve success. Adult dreams prod and poke you when you're tired, urging you to stay at work for just one more hour to get the job done right, without any flaws, and better than anyone might have expected. Adult dreams are alive and full of energy, not passive and full of demands.

If you want to succeed, you need adult dreams, free to soar unburdened by guilt, with you doing the work of chief pilot and navigator. When you've worked to achieve this level of control over your life, you'll be well prepared for the flight into the unknown that few dare attempt and at which only the perennial adolescents among us succeed.

WORKSHOP III
Stoking the Fires of Ambition

Most people assume that ambition is something you are born with, like blue eyes or big feet. That's regrettable because it leaves you with the feeling that if you, your children or spouse are deficient in the commodity of ambition, you're stuck...for life. My experience tells me differently. Research on human behavior suggests that ambition can be promoted in people. Motivational consultants have earned millions each year proving the point that ambition is an acquired rather than an inherited trait.

There are two components to ambition:

1. The desire to succeed
2. The expectation to succeed

Expectation to succeed without the desire would be merely wishful thinking. Desire to succeed without the expectation would lead to enfeebled efforts as the steam would run out as soon as the first resistance was encountered and you said to yourself, "See...I knew I'd fail. It's no use trying."

How do you instill ambition in yourself, in your loved ones and in those upon whom you depend? The process has four ingredients:

1. *You must be the lens through which the success can be viewed.* Just as certain things are invisible to the naked eye but become starkly plain under a microscope or when viewed through a pair of binoculars, the potential for success may not be apparent to someone seeking it. A person may not be aware of his or her talents. There may be an expectation of certain collapse under pressure even when the same person may have withstood previous stresses quite admirably. In short, we often lose touch with our strengths. It's important to have someone to help us focus on them once again or for the first time.

2. *Jump start a person's battery if he can't get his own motor started.* Very often, a person struggling for a long time with failure just runs out of steam and can't get going again. The energy is sapped. Hope for success is gone. Even the memories of previous successes have disappeared under the shadow of more recent painful failures. He is burnt out. But not forever.

A person in such a difficulty needs another taste of success to rekindle the fires of ambition. He needs a boost to get over the inertia of chronic failure and get ambition rolling again. You can be the source of such a boost for this person. You musn't overdo it lest you foster too great a dependency on yourself or leave the person too much in awe of your own energy and accomplishments. You need to take the position, "I'll help you get started. From thereon out, you're on your own."

3. *Let them have the pride of self-rescue.* If you help a person too much, he or she may conclude, "Well, without you I'd never have found the answer. I guess I need you in my life from now on if I'm to succeed." The pain of being lost and confused must be relieved by a person's own efforts. Only then can they build the confidence and pride that will get them through the next crisis.

In my young adult years, my father used to let me have his 1952 Pontiac complete with a full tank of gas. He'd say, "Go out with your friends. Have fun. Take a trip and explore a new place. Don't worry about getting lost. As long as you have a full tank of gas, you'll always find your way home." I'd follow his advice and go on trips each weekend: north to the Laurentian Mountains; south to Plattsburgh, New York; east to the farmlands of Quebec; west to the capital city of Ottawa in my native country of Canada. On each journey, I'd follow his advice, taking side trips anytime I saw something of interest. I'd often get lost and then find my way again, able to count on the tank of gas I kept topped off at all times.

Years later, this training stood me in good stead. As a pilot, I never panicked when I strayed off course. I'd quickly reorient myself, knowing that I had plenty of reserves in my gas tank. Calmly, I'd probe the sky until I saw a familiar landmark down below from which I could get my bearings and find my way home. In difficult periods of my life, through financial difficulties and serious illnesses, I always first identified the fuel I'd need to get through the crisis, be it courage, knowledge, love and support from friends, more hard work or just more patience. Then, reinforced by a full tank of whatever I needed, I'd find my way through the crisis.

You can help people develop the stamina to succeed by giving them the scope to explore, get lost and find themselves. As in my father's training of me, you have to give them a full tank of gas and the encouragement to explore, get lost and find themselves again. After a while, they'll learn to keep their own gas tank full of anything they need.

4. *Expect success; don't demand it.* Nothing is more encouraging to someone than your expecting them to win. Nothing causes more anxiety than your demanding that they do so on your schedule rather than at their own pace.

When the home team plays at home, what's their big advantage? The fact that everyone in the crowd expects them to win. When they play away, the crowd expects them to lose. You must give those you love the home team advantage, expecting, but not demanding, success.

You know how awful a player feels when the hometown crowd, expecting victory, begins to boo when the athlete makes an error. This crowd reaction goes beyond expecting someone to win and becomes a demand. The athlete is hurt at the sudden erosion of confidence in him. "What about all my previous successes? Don't those count?" he thinks. "No," the crowd answers emphatically with a chorus of boos. "We want to know what you have done for us lately."

Expecting success from people shows that you have recognized their potential and you respect their previous accomplishments. Demanding success means that you only acknowledge the success that they can deliver to you right now, the past be damned! This will only bring resistance and rebellion and stymie motivation to succeed.

To encourage someone, maintain a continuous expectation that they will succeed. Even in the face of failure, don't let it erode. Say, "That's O.K. Nobody can win every time out. You'll do better next time."

Now, to develop your ability to stoke the fires of someone's ambitions, including your own, read the following vignettes and choose the best responses.

1.   Judy came home at night after a hard day's work at the office. She looked despondent and said to her husband, "I think it's all over for me at the company. They're about to computerize the whole accounting system. I'm a real klutz with machines. I can't even use a screwdriver. You know that, Bill. I think I'm going to hand in my resignation and look for work elsewhere."

Bill should say:

a)   "That's O.K. Judy. I'm 100% behind you. I'll help you prepare your resume."

b)   "Don't lose faith, Judy. You know you can learn to work a computer. Besides, we need your income. Think of all the payments we have to make each month. I just can't handle it without your help."

c)   "I know you can't work a screwdriver. But that's be-cause it was never too important for you to learn. Your whole field is being computerized and I know you have it in you to keep up. Remember how you once thought you'd never be able to master a general ledger?"

2.   Brian asked his dad to help him with his biology homework. "Dad," he began, "there's no way I'm ever going to get a passing grade in this course. I'm just not a scientist. You grew up with biology. You're a doctor. Could you help me study for this exam, please?"

Brian's dad should say:

a) "I'll listen to your questions, your proposed answers and ask you why you came to those conclusions. I won't tell you the answers."

b) "Let's go over the first question. Here's how I'd do it and why. Now you do the rest and consult me if you need help. I want you to think it through thoroughly before you ask me for help."

c) "Getting out of this jam by yourself will be very helpful to you in later life. Don't bother me."

3. William was about to take a job on the West Coast. He had some trepidations. "What if I don't make friends? What if I can't find a good place to live? Do you really think I should accept this promotion and transfer?"

His best friend, Andrew, should say:

a) "Billy, I'll always be here for you if you want to pick up the phone and call. I'll put you in touch with a buddy of mine on the coast who can show you around. You'll do fine, I know it. Even if you're lonely for a while, you'll get over it. Don't let the fears you have stop you from taking the promotion."

b) "No job is so important that you should give up your lifestyle, friends and family for it. I'd stay here in New London and wait for a better spot to open up."

c) "It's going to be awfully lonely for you out there in California. I turned down a transfer there myself last year for that very reason. I think I'll ask my boss if I can transfer out there, now that I know you might go. I was too scared to go there on my own, but both of us together will do fine."

4. Donna was about to audition for a role in a soap opera. She knew the part was a real plum. She turned to her teacher for encouragement, since the competition for the part promised to be fierce.

Her drama coach should say:

a) "The chances of getting this role, even for an accomplished actress, are very slim. Don't get your hopes up too high."

b) "Don't let me down, Donna. I've put years of effort into you."

c) "You have everything it takes to do this role. You're

going to face competition. I know you'll give it your best. You always have in the past. I'm behind you all the way."

Now, what were your answers? Here are the correct ones:

1) c
2) b
3) a
4) c

In the first vignette, Judy's husband in (a) would have simply endorsed her fear of failure. In (b), although he said she could learn to operate a computer, he didn't say why. He only gave her guilt as a motivation to learn how. In (c), he gave her both encouragement and acted as a lens through which she could focus on her inner resources. "After all," said he, "there was a time when you thought you would never master a general ledger and you did."

In the second vignette, Brian's dad in (a) offered to help him to learn to reason, but didn't recognize that Brian needed a battery boost to overcome his fear of tackling the difficult course. In (c), he simply sloughed off the whole problem by telling Brian that hard knocks would help him in later life. In (b), Dad offered a head start by showing Brian how to do the first question as well as how to reason in the subject. After that, he offered to act as a consultant, giving Brian the message that he knew his son could follow his example.

In the third vignette, Billy's friend, in (b), simply helped Billy rationalize his fear of going out to the coast. No encouragement was given for Billy to use his own resources to survive. In (c), his friend confessed his own fear of going, giving Billy the message that going to California was, indeed, a scary proposition and something he better not undertake on his own. In (a), Billy's friend told him that he'd give him his first tank of gas: contact with his buddy in California, and liberal support on the telephone. After that, he encouraged Billy to learn to overcome his loneliness and assured him that he knew Billy would figure out how to make the move a success.

In the fourth vignette, the drama coach gave Donna a prophecy of gloom and doom in (a). In (b), she laid a guilt trip on Donna by trying to motivate her through saying, "Don't let me down," as if Donna was putting her ego on the line for her teacher and not for the sake of her own career. In (c), the response was encouraging and appropriate. Her drama coach reminded her that, in the past, she had always given it her best. Despite the competition, she knew Donna would persevere and use her talents well.

Ambition is a durable trait you can instill in those you love and care for. You can also strengthen your own ambition by following the advice outlined in this workshop and applying it to yourself. You can be the lens through which to see your hidden resources. You can get a jump start for a dead battery by asking friends for a boost when you feel down and out. If you feel your endurance has run dry, you can replenish your own gas tank by identifying the resources you need to cope and getting a fresh supply on your own or with the help of friends. And, last, you must never forget your track record of previous successes, especially in the face of possible failure. Only by keeping in mind what you have already accomplished can you face failure, survive it and go on to renewed successes.

WORKSHOP IV
Making a Good Thing Last

There is much to be learned from these old sayings, "He won the battle but lost the war," or, "The operation was successful but the patient died." When it comes to the search for success, the short term tactic never works as well as the long-term strategic plan.

What goes into success determines very much what its products will be. If you put in impatience, you will get out transient results. If ego and bravado go in, superficial achievement comes back. If you invest deliberate, patient caring about what you do, stability of achievement is the reward. If depth of purpose rather than ego is committed to the project, rock solid foundations are laid for long-term success.

Success is like a computer to which you can't lie. It measures every input. Then it computes and feeds back exactly what it was programmed to produce from the inputs it received. Let's assess the inputs you program into your success drive. Answer the following statements true or false.

1. I judge people by their achievements more than by their intentions.
2. The end justifies the means when it comes to success in a career.

3. I often know when people want to cheat me by the look on their face.
4. I'd rather hire a person with pride who doesn't know anything about the job than an expert who lacks self-assurance.
5. I have a lot of pride. I don't let anyone ever get away with pushing me around, no matter what the circumstances.
6. It's often better to forget about and leave a bad situation quickly than to dwell on it, trying to find the reasons why it went sour.
7. If I don't know something too well, I can often carry the day with a confident bluff.
8. It's wrong to sell someone on your dreams. You owe them the respect to let them know how chancy the proposition really is.
9. I'd rather be successful than anything else in life.
10. Success can be a trap if you forget about the rest of your life.

Answers

1. True. You're kidding yourself if you think people are judged by their good intentions more than by the results of their actions. Remember the old adage about the "road to hell?" Generally, a successful person is someone who can resist the sentimental position of giving credit to someone for his or her "good intentions" and insists, instead, on judging people by the substance of their achievement.

2. False. The end does not justify the means, especially when success is concerned. Short term expediency can become a way of life for some. It is those people we learn to mistrust in the long run and with whom we are unwilling to do business.

3. False. "Gut reaction" is the most overrated instinct in the world. If you think someone is about to or has already cheated you, don't come to a conclusion in silence and act on that belief based on facial expressions. Confront the person or gather more information over a period of time. Snap

judgments lead to quick mistakes that can be costly.

4. True. If there is a choice between pride and skill, choose pride all the time. Someone with pride will always turn out to be a craftsman when given a chance to learn. Even if someone possesses a skill, his or her achievements will never far exceed the limits set by low self-confidence.

5. False. Ego is often mistaken for pride. Often the results are disastrous. If you must fight back on all occasions with a knee-jerk response, that is a product of a swollen ego rather than actual pride. There is a time and place for fighting back: namely when the battle can be won and is worth winning. Pride accepts defeat when the circumstances don't justify the fight. Ego never does.

6. False. If you tend to move on rapidly after each mistake, you are being motivated by an ego that can't endure the shame of a mistake long enough to grow from its lessons. Naturally, you will be condemned to reliving your mistakes, just as the old proverb states.

7. False. If you don't know something, face the fact and confess your limitation. Your adversaries will respect you for it. Your friends will forgive you. Your future will reward you for having admitted the limitation. Having a habit of bluffing your way through a crisis may perfume the present but it will weaken the future.

8. False. It's perfectly honest to sell someone else on your dream. After all, if you have confidence in your abilities, that dream will most likely become a reality. If you can sell someone on your dream and add his or her energies to your own, the dream will be that much closer to a reality.

9. True. If you want to be a success, you have to value succeeding more than anything in the world. It doesn't have to be your philosophy. You may choose to value other things in life more than success. But, for those who want success badly, it must come first, above all else.

10. True. Success, even if it is your first choice, must not be your only choice. If you neglect every other aspect of your life you will run out of fuel in a crisis. It has been clearly shown that people with a strong personal life and hobbies they enjoy are far more stable under stress than those whose

lives are centered only around their work.

If you want to be a long-term winner rather than a flash in the pan, be guided by your results on this test. Realign your priorities according to what you have learned in this workshop and you will reap rewards that last a lifetime.

WORKSHOP V
What's Your Game?

One piece of advice that winning sports teams follow all the time is to make the other team play your game. Forcing a person to operate out of his or her element is disconcerting and gives you the edge you might need to win in a tough competition. Taking this good advice and turning it around, it's important to discover what, in fact, is the most favorable environment for your success.

In this regard, two dimensions of study have been productive:

1. *Are you a right- or a left-brain person?* Are you more creative and imaginative or more analytical and administrative? Your style of thinking and problem-solving has a great bearing on your success. It's not wise to assume that the job you do now taps the correct side of your brain. You might, indeed, be a right-brain person in a left-brain job. In fact, the neuropsychological equivalent of The Peter Principle might be stated as follows: "Every job calls on a person to specialize in the use of one given side of the brain. Every promotion puts you in a new job that forces you to use the side of the brain opposite to the one that qualified you for the promotion."

An example of this would be the person who is a wonderfully creative talent and whose accomplishments are rewarded by a promotion to an administrative role as vice president. The promotion requires a shift from predominantly right-brain creative activity to left-brain administrative duties. Naturally, the new job would be performed with less skill, leading to less likelihood that future promotions would be forthcoming. Hence the Peter Principle would operate with people rising to a level of incompetence, unable to advance further in the organization. The same would be true of an administrative type who got ahead in left-brain skills and who is handed a whole division to manage and is now expected to be creative with the product line and marketing strategy. Faced with significant right-brain demands, that person might founder and fail to advance as quickly as when he was only asked to administer and analyze as he had done in the previous job.

It's important to recognize whether you are predominantly a right- or left-brain person and to rely on the skills of that disposition to a maximum. If you are promoted to or faced with demands that draw on the side of the brain that is your weaker one, use a consultant's or subordinate's abilities to supplement your own.

2. *Are you a team player or a solo competitor?* Research has shown that the one place where there is a strong divergence of personality traits in winners is between team versus solo competitors. If you are suited to one form of competition, you must stick to that mode for best results.

Solo competitors tend to be introverted, dominant, non-nurturant and have low empathy. Team players are found to be more extroverted, self-effacing, needy of nurturing and capable of nurturing others and highly empathic. Some of these traits can be learned, allowing you ultimately to succeed at an endeavor for which you were originally not suited.

Consultants to industry have reaped fortunes selling programs which enhance empathy (such as T-Group training); teaching people to be outgoing (Dale Carnegie being a good example); and fostering a more self-effacing, cooperative approach to corporate life (training in how to listen to others being one example). Business recognizes the need for team players. It also knows that those who rise to the top may have gotten there through skills that helped them succeed at solo, head-to-head competition. Making the transition from solo competitor to team player is a crucial requirement for high level managerial success.

To analyze your skills and find out whether you are a right- or left-brain thinker or a solo or individual competitor take the following test. Answer true or false to the statements that best describe your behavior or attitudes:

T   F

1. I judge people's potential by the organization and clarity of the reports they submit.
2. My heart pounds when I have to speak up in a large crowd.
3. In trying to solve a problem, I like to break it down into components and then attack each one one at a time.
4. I find that I get a job done better when I don't have interference from people who want to put their two cents in.
5. I get really annoyed when people "shoot from the hip" in trying to solve problems.
6. Work is a place for getting a job done and not for seeking sympathy.
7. Most often, a solution to a problem comes to me in a flash of insight rather than through systematic analysis.
8. I am often described as the life of the party or as one of the "in" crowd.
9. I love messing around with ideas and turning them upside down.
10. My successes have had a lot to do with the input I got from others.
11. I am quite artistic.
12. I feel a responsibility to help out when I notice a friend is upset, even if that person would rather not open up.
13. I pride myself in being able to capture the essence of a problem and am not as good on the follow-up details involved in implementing the solution.
14. I like work more if there is a family feeling amongst the staff.

Answers and Analysis

Left-brain traits—True on questions 1, 3, 5
False on questions 7, 9, 11, 13

Right-brain traits—False on questions 1, 3, 5
                      True on questions 7, 9, 11, 13

Solo-competitor traits—True on questions 2, 4, 6
                      False on questions 8, 10, 12, 14

Team-competitor traits—False on questions 2, 4, 6
                      True on questions 8, 10, 12, 14

If your career is well established and your personality is set for life, you may use the results of the above test to confirm your strengths and go on relying upon them in the future. However, if you haven't reached your goals either in terms of career or personality development, it is important to reflect on the results of the test and try to strengthen the traits that are found to be deficient.

The same advice can be used for people who would like to raise successful children. It's important that your children know how to succeed in solo as well as in team competition. It's crucial that they be creative as well as competently analytical and possess good administrative skills. Only then can maximum success be assured when they are faced with the variety of challenges life can pose.

Perhaps the most critical learning experience for someone who wants to acquire missing skills is having a role model to follow. The right-brain creative person needs to confess to a mentor or friend, "I need your help in learning to organize and administer my work." A left-brain person needs someone whose creativity can enliven and redirect the plodding administrative, analytical thinking so typical of left-brain people. A child with two dissimilar parents who takes after the more artistic one should be encouraged to spend more time with the more analytical one, even though there is a more natural fit with the artistic one. A person who is introverted, stubbornly dominant, non-nurturant and has little empathy needs to associate with people of opposite dispositions if he or she wants to make a switch from solo competition to being a team player.

Learning by osmosis is the most effective technique I know for rapid self-improvement. But remember, for osmosis to work in a chemical experiment, the membrane must be permeable. It must be able to breathe and let in that to which it is exposed. For you to learn by osmosis, your mind must not be impenetrable. It must accept the influences of the role model you have chosen. To teach by osmosis, you, as a role model, must win acceptance by your student. Apprenticeship, an age-old method of learning and teaching by osmosis, still has immense value for personality development. However, it cannot succeed without a receptive learner and a credible teacher.

Success, when we analyze it as we have done in this book, is a contagious process. It is transmitted from one winner to the rest of the team members; it passes down the generations from a credible parent to a pliable child; it is a fire that spreads from an energetic boss to an uncertain employee. At its core, success is nothing more than a full expansion of one's capabilities. However, to realize such an accomplishment requires knowledge of your potentials, faith that they can work for you and courage that lets you proceed without any assurance of success except that which your self-esteem lets you dare hope you will attain.

EPILOGUE

Sometimes one single person can embody all active traits, both positive and negative, of success. One man I treated some years ago represented to me the essence of the issues this book has addressed.

Arthur had already achieved the most demonstrable success one could wish to attain. He was head of a profitable company that was growing by leaps and bounds. He had taken it over from its founders years earlier and had applied his unique skills to stimulating the phenomenal growth to prominence of the business. Now, at a time when he should have been able to enjoy his achievements, he couldn't. Instead, he insisted on driving himself further and further into the workings of every aspect of the operation until his capable subordinates took one of two remedies: they rebelled against him or they quit.

Suddenly, from a smooth-running organization, he was faced with a chaotic rebellion and a defection of his most talented executives to his competitors or into their own business. Arthur wouldn't relent. He persisted in trying to do everything himself until he suffered a severe anxiety attack that, I am sure, was a signal of serious overload of his mind and body. He had ignored the early warning sign of labored breathing (a feeling of not being able to get enough oxygen with every breath) until it resulted in a full-fledged panic attack with heart palpitations and a feeling of impending doom. What had Arthur done wrong? He wanted to know the answer to this question and so did I.

Reviewing all his S-Factor traits, it was clear that his errors were all due to the exaggeration of these traits, not due to a deficiency of any one of them.

- He loved controlling his destiny. This was right up the alley of an S-Factor person. However, he couldn't share the least bit of control with others or let subordinates expand their own skills by being given more responsibility. Hence, they finally rebelled.
- He had high self-esteem, but in Arthur's case it was so high that, like a cancer, it grew without restraint or respect for those around, choking off the self-esteem of others in the process.
- He was tough-minded and stuck to his guns, just as someone with the S-Factor is supposed to do. But Arthur couldn't let others get a word or idea in edgewise. Hence, his steamroller personality drove talented subordinates to frustration and then into the hands of his competitors.
- He was extroverted, just as a good team player is supposed to be, but Arthur needed the stage at all times. Extroversion is highly useful in teamwork since it enhances cooperation to have good communicators on the team. Arthur's signals could be heard by all. But other voices in the organization fell on his deaf ears.
- While Arthur was intelligent and creative, traits that had allowed him to single-handedly raise a small company into the big leagues, he insisted on overpowering others with these strengths. His subordinates wouldn't be scolded for making a mistake. He'd simply take over the project and do it the right way, taking on task after task that others could not perform with the ease and adeptness he could. Consequently, only Arthur's creativity and intelligence saw the light of day in tangible accomplishments. His associates knew that, "If it's im-

portant, Arthur will do it himself." Consequently, those with pride, who wouldn't take this denigration, left. Others rebelled against the paternalism. Finally, it all caught up with Arthur in one massive attack of the Burnout Syndrome. He panicked, then lost his motivation to do anything in the company at all. Not having nurtured a cadre of coordinated subordinates, the organization began to fall apart.

Over the next months, I worked with Arthur to relieve his panic, to renew his enthusiasm for his work and to tone down and modulate his overpowering S-Factor personality. Arthur is now back in charge of the company. But he shares his work with a stable of young Arthurs; people who, like Arthur, are S-Factor personalities and are straining at the bit to win for themselves and for the company. As their efforts came on line at the company, Arthur was able to gear down his own, focusing his talents on the critical issues that needed his individual attention and enjoying a renewal of energy, spirit and prosperity.

S-Factor traits are a power to be reckoned with and, in the extreme, a force that can destroy the very success you seek. It is my hope that the effect of this book will be twofold: to help people actualize their potential through a focused attention to these traits I have outlined and described and to share the wealth of their accomplishments with others, acting as a mentor who can recognize S-Factor traits in someone who needs careful guidance, encouragement and a chance to learn through the exalted process of self-expression.

INDEX